Brand Vision

Brand Vision

The Clear Line of Sight Aligning Business Strategy and Marketing Tactics

Jim Everhart

BEP

BUSINESS EXPERT PRESS

Leader in applied, concise business books

Brand Vision:
The Clear Line of Sight Aligning Business Strategy and Marketing Tactics

Cover design by Divya Pidaparti

Interior design by Exeter Premedia Services Private Ltd., Chennai, India

First published in 2022 by
Business Expert Press, LLC
222 East 46th Street, New York, NY 10017
www.businessexpertpress.com

ISBN-13: 978-1-63742-173-4 (paperback)
ISBN-13: 978-1-63742-174-1 (e-book)

Business Expert Press Marketing Collection

Collection ISSN: 2169-3978 (print)
Collection ISSN: 2169-3986 (electronic)

First edition: 2022

10 9 8 7 6 5 4 3 2 1

To Celeste.
My muse, past, present, and always.

Description

In a global survey of more than four thousand senior executives, consulting firm PwC found that 80 percent of the respondents admitted that few of their associates understood their company's corporate strategy. And even that figure is wildly optimistic. According to research reported in the Harvard Business Review, 95 percent of a company's employees, on average, are unaware of or do not understand its strategy.

Brand Vision: The Clear Line of Sight Aligning Business Strategy and Marketing Tactics hopes to change that by offering simple, easily implemented tools connecting a company's marketing program to its business strategy. It's based on a critical premise: that, rather than merely a series of aesthetic decisions on typography and graphics, marketing can be a powerful force that helps a company communicate its strategy. Not just externally, but internally as well.

The author has covered this territory for more than four decades, working as a strategist, creative director, and writer for one of the country's largest business-to-business advertising agencies. He has worked with large international companies to develop marketing campaigns and programs from social media, search, e-mail, and websites to more traditional print advertising and direct marketing. He knows this territory well.

The author developed and honed these tools in countless presentations to clients, using them to help companies define their business strategy, understand their audiences, develop creative that captivates and engages, create high-impact campaigns, and measure the success of their efforts.

The author looks forward to sharing these tools with both marketing professionals and corporate executives who want their business strategies to come alive in their marketing.

Brand Vision combines Seth Godin's elegant thinking, *Guerrilla Marketing's* straightforward simplicity, and *Blue Ocean Strategy's* revolutionary approach.

Keywords

brand vision; strategic messaging; messaging strategy; brand messaging; marketing messaging; strategic branding; brand strategy; marketing strategy; pyramid messaging; brand marketing; strategic marketing; corporate strategy; communications strategy; integrated marketing; marketing integration; brand integration; marketing strategy; business strategy; marketing ROI; marketing results; marketing return on investment

Contents

Testimonials

"The tone is perfect—I feel so relaxed even as the author is bullet-pointing my EXACT pain points. It's like this book was written exactly for my company AND my role right now. Every time I turned the page I found myself saying 'YES! Exactly!' This book is a treasure."—**Bridget Reilly, VP of Content for Authentication, JPMorgan Chase & Co.**

"I don't think I've ever read a marketing book that took such a complex topic and made it easy to follow. I find it to be extremely relevant to today. There's always going to be a new social media platform or digital space to play in, but that's not what's relevant. This book gives the blueprint for relevance. Everything is laid out so clearly, I'm not sure how a marketer operating today would not find it tremendously useful. I really loved every bit of it. I also loved all the stories. They jumped out and I'm sure anyone who works in any company anywhere can identify with them. I'm going to make it required reading—and practice—for my two newbies."—**Nancy DeZarn, Senior Marketing Manager, JLG Industries**

"Really well done! It is thoughtful, to the point, and instructive for marketing practitioners like me as well as all marketing stakeholders. I like it a lot!"
—**Larry Foy, Marketing Director, Bosch Rexroth**

"A list of tactics is not a comprehensive strategy! If you are looking for an approach to help you define all the aspects of having a strong approach to business strategy down into the marketing funnel, Jim Everhart deftly guides you through the interlocking world of the pyramid. It's easier than you thought to have a strong foundation, connecting the dots across audiences and channels and making sure your marketing campaign is effective!"
—**Lynne M. Demers-Hunt, Divisional Marketing Communications Director, Fenner Precision Polymers**

"*B2B marketing professionals are increasingly under pressure to deliver measurable results. Not clicks, impressions, MQLs, but genuine revenue attribution. The first step in that process is understanding your audience, your markets, your value proposition, etc. and then tailoring your creative and your messaging accordingly. What's especially unique about* Brand Vision *is that not only has Jim offered several personal examples and diagrams to make these concepts 'sticky,' but he's actually provided several useful templates, too, which makes this book immediately actionable.*"—**Lance Baird, Ringleader, RIVET, Demand Generation for Industrial Markets**

"*Brand Vision is the roadmap I've been waiting for. And it's just plain fun to have such a knowledgeable and companiable guide as Jim Everhart to lead the journey. Finally, I can see it! This book is PRICELESS! Thank you, Jim!*"
—**Catharine Oakes Hollenbach, Runningpump Marketing**

Acknowledgments

I want to thank my family, of course, for putting up with me during the writing process. Ben, Tina, and Kiran; Blake, Rachel, and Connor. And, of course, my wife Celeste.

I'd like to thank my intrepid band of reviewers, Larry Foy, Nancy Carl, Lynne Demers-Hunt, Lance Baird, Bridget Reilly, and Catharine Oakes Hollenbach for their comments and honest criticism. They often say how important reviewers are, and writers often nod in agreement, but forge ahead solo. That has been my practice all too often in the past but won't be in the future. Honestly, I took every one of their comments to heart. And though I may not have done exactly as they suggested, I made substantive revisions as a result. Thanks to all.

I'd also like to thank the hundreds or even thousands of clients, coworkers, and collaborators who have worked with me in the decades of my writing, publishing, advertising, production, and marketing career. I have always marveled at the intelligence and creativity of the people who work in these spheres. They have helped me become a better writer and strategist.

And, finally, I'd like to thank my brother, Dr. Charles W. Everhart Jr., who got me started on this journey several decades ago by giving me a copy of *Guerilla Marketing*.

Introduction

It was late in the day when I received a frantic call from an account manager at the business-to-business (B2B) agency where I worked. The client's president and CEO was demanding a "clear line of sight" between business strategies and marketing tactics. How, they wanted to know, would a specific tactic—like a trade show, brochure, or video—help the company achieve its strategic goals? Things like value innovation or global reach.

The request was not that unusual. American companies each year spend billions of dollars in business planning and strategy. Yet, in a global survey of 4,400 senior executives,[1] consulting firm PwC found that about 80 percent of the respondents admitted that their overall corporate strategy was not well understood, even within their own companies. And that means they're not implemented, especially in marketing, where strategy needs to come to life if it's going to be effective.

It's a sad truth that business strategy often gets lost in the fog of marketing warfare as the abundance of new choices inundates marketers. Things such as websites, public relations (PR) releases, ads, e-mails, paid search, or Facebook posts take on a life of their own, demanding immediate action, and paying little heed to the grand strategy. And they all claim to be silver bullets.

Every year, there are thousands of articles and millions of words written about creating business strategies. Plus, there are hundreds of books published.

Brand Vision is not one of them. It is not a blueprint for creating a strategy. Rather it is a clarion call to implement the strategy you already have.

Maybe you'll need help discovering the strategy you already have. Or articulating it clearly. That's fine. We'll get to that.

---

[1] P. Leinwand and C. Mainardi. 2016. "Creating a Strategy that Works," *Strategy + Business*. www.strategy-business.com/feature/Creating-a-Strategy-That-Works

What Brand Vision Is

Brand Vision is designed to be a practical, step-by-step program that provides a solid framework for implementing business strategies through the marketing process. It uses strategic messaging to connect business strategy and marketing tactics, giving corporate executives and marketers the lens they need to sharpen their focus, clarify their objectives, and bring their goals in sight. It is about making those vital connections between business strategy and marketing tactics. Bridging those divides.

In other words, it's designed to give our client's CEO the clear line of sight that exec was looking for.

How Will It Help You?

As noted earlier, there are tons of people who want to tell marketers how to do strategy their way. But when it comes to the hard, day-to-day work of *implementing* it in the real world, they're nowhere to be found.

Brand Vision is all about giving both corporate marketers and agency people the tools to implement the company's strategy in their day-to-day activities. It provides you:

- A guidebook out of the chaos, making sure marketing tactics aligns with business strategy and objectives.
- A plan to develop strategic messaging that connects strategy to tactics … and drives all your communications.
- A way to relate your company's business strategies to your marketing campaigns, branding, and even your blog and Facebook posts.
- A clear understanding of marketing principles and how they apply in the age of Google, Facebook, and Twitter.
- The ammunition to go to your bosses and not simply justify your existing marketing budget but ask for more.
- The opportunity to be taken seriously at your companies, giving you a seat at the table.
- The tools to maximize marketing investments. To stop frittering away marketing resources and put them where they will

have maximum impact on your company, its products, and
your career.

- A shared lexicon marketers and agency people can use to
communicate with each other and explain strategy-driven
campaigns to their clients (external and internal).
- The chance to end destructive debates about colors, logos,
graphics, tactics, marketing tools, and creative executions.
In effect, an escape from the "sandbox," the tendency to view
marketing and creative as a place to play.

Best of all, *Brand Vision* provides clear direction on how to make sense
of all the reams of data now available, thereby transforming marketing into a
data-driven enterprise. Helping you know what to expect from a marketing
program. Turning analytics from a reactive exercise (about what did or didn't
happen) into a predictive tool. Knowing what to expect from individual marketing tactics. And what *not* to expect. And making marketing more about
data than aesthetics, knowing what data to look at (and what to ignore).

Why Marketers Need This Book

Brand Vision provides a comprehensive overview connecting high-level
business strategy with individual tactics such as social media, blogs, white
papers, ads, and news articles.

It gives you practical help in addressing your day-to-day struggles.
It shows you how to sort through the dizzying array of tactics available
to you. Answering questions like, what's the best way to promote a new
product? How do you launch a brand? How will you know if a program
has been successful? What's better, display or search advertising? And,
most importantly, how do you show your bosses that the company benefits from marketing? And show them why they should give you even more
money in your next budget?

What's in It for Your Boss?

Increasingly, business leaders recognize the need to bridge the gap between
marketing and their corporate strategy.

First, they want their overall strategy to succeed. And they believe, quite rightly, that marketing can help them achieve that success.

Second, they are beginning to recognize that customers are not all equal. They no longer expect marketing simply to bring in customers of all shapes and sizes. They expect marketing to help the company land customers who are buying what the corporation is selling. People who are not looking for the lowest price, but who want the unique advantages the company offers and are willing to pay for them.

Third, they understand that marketing can help them change or enhance the perception of the company. Though they may be happy with their company's current positioning, forward-looking executives understand they may need to change in the future, with speed and agility. *Brand Vision* marketing gives them the flexibility and messaging power to reach all their audiences, both external and internal.

And fourth, by harnessing everyone's efforts to the corporate strategy, *Brand Vision* may help bridge the yawning gap between marketing and sales, both resolutely camped in their respective silos. Implementation of the *Brand Vision* process, using agreed-upon tools and language, should help close that divide.

Marketers will be equipped to position their discipline not as an expense but as a value-added resource. One that can help a company launch new products more efficiently, lower customer acquisition costs, command a premium price, carve out higher margins, energize channels, communicate better internally and externally, and even enhance stockholder value.

Over a 40-year career, I have practiced strategy-driven marketing and messaging. And, for more than 30 years, I have developed and used the tools outlined in this book to integrate, implement, and execute business strategies in marketing tactics.

Why Pyramids?

Each of the five parts of this book builds a pyramid device that illustrates the concepts presented. Pyramids have a universal, almost exotic appeal. They define a plane, also illustrating the rule of three. They symbolize deductive reasoning: proceeding from several different ideas to a single, overarching summary concept, made more powerful through the reasoning process.

I first saw the potential of pyramids as a method to organize corporate messaging in the late 1980s, when I was introduced to hyperlinking. Then I used it to explain to a client how to organize messaging at different levels. It became so successful that Godfrey Advertising, the agency where I worked at the time, made the pyramid a prominent part of its service and even used it as part of its logo. For many years, the agency took every new client through a day-long pyramid-building exercise. I led most of the first sessions, conducting a total of more than one hundred for clients over the years.

I experimented with the other pyramids at various times over the years. But it wasn't until I had worked with this project for several months that I developed the more advanced *Brand Vision* process, discovering the clear line of sight they create from strategy to return on investment (ROI). I realized then how helpful this book would be for corporate executives who want their plans executed at the tactical level. And for marketing professionals (both in companies and agencies) who need a common language and messaging to communicate a company's strategic vision and drive marketing efforts from high-level ads and web pages to e-mails and tweets.

I have seen this approach work time and again. For more than a decade, people at all levels of Godfrey used pyramid language (a high-level positioning piece was a "top of the pyramid" tactic) to communicate about a particular project. And the agency experienced remarkable growth during that period.

More importantly, these pyramids were all developed in response to a specific client problem, concern, or issue I have seen over the years. As a result, most chapters will feature at least one client anecdote. Something you will most likely have heard in your own company.

Connecting the Dots

Upon completing this book, you will have a road map connecting all the dots: business strategy, audiences, messaging, campaigns, and results. Actually, it's a pyramid, several of them. And, taken together, they give you a clear line of sight from business strategy to marketing tactics.

PART I

Strategy: Insight That Activates

Brand Vision starts with strategy. Admittedly, it's a thorny subject. In all too many companies, strategy becomes a political football. Top management wants to dictate it. The ambitious want to own it. Salesmen think it's about beating competitors on every pitch. New managers want to change it (whether it's working or not).

Often confused with mission and vision, which can be aspirational, strategy needs to be concrete. *Actionable!* All too often, the opposite is true. We've all heard of business strategies relegated to a shelf or desk drawer, never to be seen again.

Strategists themselves often don't help. They sometimes revel in abstractions. Reach agreement by caving in to entrenched interests. Indulge people who think the company needs to be all things to all people. When nothing is further from the truth.

Admittedly, the marketer who would connect to a company's business strategy is in a difficult spot, often being torn in different directions.

On the one hand, high-level executives, most often represented by those developing mission statements, promote an all-inclusive, universal view. They'll typically promote the importance of people. Sustainability. Empowerment. Inclusiveness. Corporate social responsibility. Those are all great and worthy goals for companies to emulate. But they are not competitive strategies.

On the other hand, we have the sales organization. Sometimes, they want marketers to emphasize price. Essentially, making their job easier. But more often, they like the all-inclusive, universal view, because it gives them tons of room to maneuver. And be whatever a customer wants them (and your company) to be. If that means they sell to Customer A on price and Customer B on product quality and Customer C on close customer care, so be it. They'll take the money and run.

The corporate marketer, however, needs to become the C-level's best hope of advancing a logical, well-thought-out business strategy, both internally and externally. Telling the audience what to expect and helping the troops make decisions all up and down the line that reinforce that strategy and make it real.

Definitions

Some of the problem with strategy starts with the word itself and its current cachet. I've been in meetings where people throw the term around to describe their plans for everything from PR and search to Instagram and e-mail.

Let's agree from the outset that those things can and should be strategic. But they are not strategies themselves. Strategy is a notoriously binary choice: Either you have one or you don't. And having five is the same as not having one at all.

Here's why. When you say you have a strategy for something like Instagram, you're trying to say you're not suggesting something haphazard. That the things you are proposing are important, well worth the effort. And that you have a plan that has been thought out, considered carefully. You may even have tried to outline the business case, proving the company will benefit. That's all well and good.

But you're also saying something else, directly or indirectly. You're saying that your Instagram plan is so important, it doesn't need to coordinate, complement, or play well with anything else your company is doing. It's new. It's too important, too special. It doesn't have to work with your advertising. It's too critical to fit into your marketing program. And yes, it's even more important than your business strategy. It's above all that.

Sorry, I'm not buying that.

That's something your company simply can't allow. Your business strategy is too important. If there's one thing the experts agree on, it's that.

Strategy Requires Hard Choices

Despite all the confusion and hand-wringing, a good strategy is not really that hard to figure out. But it is, almost by definition, notoriously hard to implement.

It involves making difficult choices and sticking with them. It requires concerted effort and diligent execution. It doesn't necessarily involve brilliance, but rather courage. Honesty. Integrity.

But most of all, it deserves clarity. Strategy should *not* be esoteric, abstract, or confusing. Rather, it needs to be crystal clear, even intuitive. Orit Gadiesh and James L. Gilbert[1] note in their 80–100 rule, a strategy that is 80 percent right and 100 percent implemented is better than a strategy that is 100 percent right and not understood (or implemented).

It is what helps a company unite behind a shared vision. There can be dissent, of course. But about tactics, implementation. Not core principles.

All too often, special interests throughout the organization—from sales and product management to C-level executives—shrink from making the required sacrifices. That is the greatest obstacle to strategy. And even business success.

A clear strategy is critical to the marketing process, providing the substance, the spirit behind all your communications. Staying on message is a lot easier when you actually have one.

Identifying the right course is easy. Living with the choice is what is hard. You owe that to your stakeholders: workers, customers, partners, and stockholders alike.

Not a New Approach

The goal here is not to offer a new approach to strategy. There are plenty of great choices out there. Rather it is to understand what a strategy is, how it works, and how it needs to be applied to marketing.

This book also will offer some tools to apply that strategy across your entire marketing program, from positioning and branding to social media posts and paid search. And it will outline a process to identify, promote, implement, and live the strategy you have, along with a way to evaluate your success at doing so.

---

[1] O. Gadiesh and J.L. Gilbert. 2001. "Transforming Corner-Office Strategy into Frontline Action," *HBR's 10 Must Reads on Strategy* (Including Featured Article "What Is Strategy?" by Michael E. Porter), 128. Boston: Harvard Business Review Press. Kindle Edition.

CHAPTER 1

Positioning: Who Are You?

Chapter Overview

The positioning inherent in your business strategy needs to drive all marketing initiatives. The good news is that most companies have one. The bad news is that many companies do not articulate it clearly. The process of defining and expressing that positioning is critical to marketing.

Who Are You?

Business strategy answers a fundamental question: "Who are you?" It identifies your core purpose. And it establishes your positioning, the central dynamic for marketing.

Unfortunately, positioning sometimes gets lost in the shuffle, as the pressure of everyday life causes us to sometimes lose sight of what is important.

But it is critical for marketing because your brand needs to embody it. Your social media needs to express it. Your products need to align with it. Your website needs to live it. You ignore it at your peril.

The Good News: You Probably Have One

The good news is that, for well or ill, most companies have a positioning. Actually, everyone has one, whether they know it or not. Usually, it is programmed into a company's DNA. It may have begun with a founder or early visionary. Then it might have gone underground as the company's early leaders hired like-minded people, who held the same assumptions, worked with the same customers, and followed the same processes and practices.

More importantly, your customers usually know it. At least, they know why they buy from you, even if you don't. They have strong feelings about whether you're the industry innovator. The price leader. Or the customer affinity pro.

So it's there. It may not be well articulated. Perhaps it's just assumed that everyone knows it. And therein lies a potential problem.

The Bad News: It May Not Be Spelled Out

The bad news is that companies often don't articulate their positioning. It may be so ingrained, people stop repeating or referring to it. They don't spell it out. It's no longer front and center where it needs to be. And they may even forget about it.

There are problems with that strong, silent approach, especially when there is a significant amount of turnover, or when a company's founders are replaced by the next generation. The new people simply don't know, haven't heard, haven't lived the positioning the way the first generation did.

A related problem occurs when the positioning is viewed as obvious. The assumption is that "Everyone knows it."

The point is that they don't. And, over time, even the best positioning starts getting fuzzy. First, internally, subtly. And it's only a matter of time before it gets fuzzy externally as well. Sales reps start selling on price or over-service their accounts. Or the company starts giving away a core strength, in order to build volume. And that is a problem.

Even worse, the positioning begins to be viewed as a description of reality. For everyone. As if the company's way of doing something is the *only* way that task can be accomplished. And competitive differentiation does not exist.

The assumption is that "everybody does it this way." And it's impossible to conceive of any other way to do your core tasks. Your company might, for example, believe that the only way to market its products is through distributors. The decision was made years, even decades ago. And while that may have been the best choice then, things change. And the belief that your company's present practice is the only viable alternative is short-sighted and dangerous.

That kind of thinking sets the stage for some nasty competitive surprises, especially in an age of disruption.

And while marketing is usually targeted primarily at external audiences, it plays an absolutely critical role with those all-important internal audiences as well—where positioning isn't simply some words or a slogan. It needs to be second nature. Your lifeblood. A good reason to come to work in the morning.

Failing to clearly articulate and promote your positioning can thus set in motion a dangerous chain of events. Where your people don't know what your positioning is or how it applies to your day-to-day operations. And marketing misses the opportunity to bring it to life on your website, PR releases, ads, e-mails, paid search, or Facebook posts.

The worst-case scenario is when the strategy process becomes captive. When CEOs want to impress their peers by embracing the latest trend, whether it's environmental policy, inclusivity, or globalism. Or on the opposite extreme, when a sales-oriented exec focuses on the particular wants, needs, or obsessions of a vocal customer, leading to a fixation on price or customer rebates.

Strategy and Positioning

Harvard professor Michael Porter is credited with kicking off the modern focus on strategy with his 1980 work *Competitive Strategy*. In a work that has become mandatory reading for MBA students, Porter provides a framework of logic about how a few key inputs define how a business prospers.

A number of other authors have made major contributions. Jim Collins said a company should have a "hedgehog concept" in *Good to Great*[2] and, previously, when collaborating with Jerry Porras, talked about a core ideology or core purpose.[3]

---

[2] J.C. Collins. 2011. *Good to Great*. New York, NY: Harper Business.

[3] J.C. Collins and J.I. Porras. 1996. "Building Your Company's Vision," *HBR's 10 Must Reads on Strategy (including featured article "What Is Strategy?" by Michael E. Porter)*, 53–54. Boston: Harvard Business Review Press. Kindle Edition.

Michael Treacy and Fred Wiersma took Porter's work and went one step further, suggesting[4] that there were three main positioning strategies (they called them "value disciplines") a company could use to differentiate itself: product leadership, operational excellence, and customer affinity.

Product/Technology Leadership

A product/technology leadership company is acknowledged as the clear leader in product development and the associated technology. Treacy and Wiersma's examples at the time included SONY, but we would now automatically think of Apple or BMW.

Strategy experts have debated whether innovation should be in a category of its own, separate from product leadership. While that was all the rage a few years ago when everyone wanted to be an innovator, it has subsided somewhat. In large measure, because product leaders don't stay on top without constant research and reinvention.

Operational Excellence

The operational excellence company's skill at production, execution, and delivery is state-of-the-art, allowing it to be either the price leader in the market (think Walmart) or the leader in delivering high production quality. Chemical companies come to mind here, because of the dire consequences when there is a "problem" with the purity of a chemical.

And while operational considerations are important, there can be a problem. Porter noted[5] that some companies allow management tools such as total quality management (TQM) or continuous improvement to overtake strategy. As managers push for operational effectiveness, he said, they implement incremental changes in products, try to serve broader customer groups,

---

[4] M. Treacy and F. Wiersma. 1994. *The Discipline of Market Leaders: Choose Your Customers, Narrow Your Focus, Dominate Your Market.* Reading, MA: Addison-Wesley Publishing.

[5] M.E. Porter. 1996. "What Is Strategy?" *HBR's 10 Must Reads on Strategy (including featured article "What Is Strategy?" by Michael E. Porter)*, 3–4. Harvard Business Review Press. Kindle Edition.

or imitate competitors (usually described as benchmarking or following industry best practices). In doing so, they sometimes drift away from their competitive positioning. Companies can only find their way back to their core positioning by removing these almost imperceptible changes that have clustered, like barnacles (Porter's term) on otherwise sound organizations.

Customer Affinity

A company in customer affinity mode almost wraps itself around its customer to deliver exactly what they want. A "Have it your way" mindset, if you will. Logistics companies like UPS, especially, fit this model well.

Customer affinity, however, is not the same as being customer focused, which really isn't a strategy as much as a way of life. The reason it's not a strategy is that it is not differentiating: *everyone* needs to focus on customers, no matter what their positioning. It's just that a product leadership company meets customer needs in ways that are different from an operational excellence company.

This positioning also doesn't mean that a company needs to meet *all* of a customer's needs. While the thought is admirable, it's neither strategic nor sustainable. Rather, a company must focus on those activities that are truly differentiating.

Focus on One, Competent in All Three

While every company needs to be at least competent in all three areas, they need to distinguish themselves by focusing their time, effort, and resources in one of these areas.

Trying to match best practices in all three areas, Porter famously wrote a few years back, is a recipe for mediocrity. A company that tries to be all things to all people probably will generate confusion among customers ... and even compromise their credibility.

"The essence of strategy," Porter wrote,[6] "is choosing what not to do."

---

[6] M.E. Porter. 1996. "What is Strategy?" *HBR's 10 Must Reads on Strategy (including featured article "What Is Strategy?" by Michael E. Porter)*, 17. Boston: Harvard Business Review Press. Kindle Edition.

Trying to straddle more than one positioning doesn't work either, he wrote. At the agency I worked at, we once had a debate about whether a company could claim "value" as their positioning, meaning the idea that its products were neither the best nor the cheapest, but a great compromise between the two. I thought about the idea but realized the problem: While this "middle ground" approach might have short-term attractiveness, it is clearly not distinguishing or differentiating. More importantly, it is not sustainable. It could easily be attacked or imitated, especially by competitors from low-cost countries. It is a prescription for intense competition and low margins, landing a company squarely in the "red ocean" of bloody, hand-to-hand combat W. Chan Kim and Renée Mauborgne described in *Blue Ocean Strategy*.[7]

To Porter, the essence of strategic positioning is choosing a tailored set of activities that make it extremely difficult for competitors to emulate. The better the "fit" among those activities, the harder they are to imitate. And thus, the positioning is more sustainable. As a result, Porter defines strategy itself quite simply as creating fit among a company's activities.

For me, one of the key questions that makes the choice very stark is this one: If you suddenly had a million dollars in investment capital, what would you do with it? Hire sales and customer service people? Build a new factory? Add some brilliant new scientists? Pay off debt?

The nonstrategic answer is that you try to do all of those. I have seen companies try to do that. The results are poor. Investing the money wisely, to build competitive differentiation, makes your position harder and harder to imitate and builds long-term success.

The message is quite simple: You cannot be all things to all people. And trying to do that makes you weaker in the long term.

Some critics have argued that Porter's insistence on sustainable competitive advantage is too limiting, that there are a number of new factors, such as social media or the ongoing digital revolution, which change the rules of the game.

---

[7] W.C. Kim and R. Mauborgne. 2015. *Blue Ocean Strategy: How to Create Uncontested Market Space and Make the Competition Irrelevant.* Boston: Harvard Business School Publishing.

They have advocated for greater agility and flexibility, arguing that competitive advantage is transient at best and advancing ideas like lean start-ups and the idea that especially new companies are essentially searching for a business model.

In my view, that's not how things work. When mankind first landed on the moon in 1969, a lot of things changed. Computers took a huge step forward, for instance. But some things didn't change. We still need to obey the laws of gravity, even though we changed our understanding of the subject, to say the least.

The same is true of marketing. Yes, Facebook, Twitter, Instagram, and especially the Internet and e-mail have changed the way we go to market. But the rules are still the same. We simply have different tools.

Most people understand the rules. They just think they apply to everyone else. Their business or industry is so different, so unique, they say, the rules don't apply. They start to believe their own hype, that "this changes everything."

There may be some instances in which that is the case. Where a company, in effect, repeals the laws of gravity. And those situations are remarkable, indeed. But, in doing this work for more than four decades, I haven't seen one yet.

The point is, the rules apply. You probably aren't special, you're just too close to see things clearly.

You need someone to tell you that. I just did.

The Benefits of a Solid Positioning

When a company adopts a clear positioning that is widely understood internally and externally, decision making is improved. Employee retention and even loyalty is increased, and the company begins to attract like-minded people. A sense of clarity settles in.

As Chris Zook and James Allen[8] discovered in their research, a straightforward strategy, structured around differentiation, not only

---

[8] C. Zook and J. Allen. 2011. "The Great Repeatable Business Model," *HBR's 10 Must Reads on Strategy, Vol. 2 (with bonus article "Creating Shared Value" By Michael E. Porter and Mark R. Kramer)*, 128. Boston: Harvard Business Review Press. Kindle Edition.

benefits customers but internal stakeholders. When employees fully understand a company's positioning, they act in concert, adapting to changing situations more easily than do competitors. They documented that such companies achieved remarkable performance and termed a company's sources of differentiation its "crown jewels."

In addition, Clayton Christensen, who introduced the concept of disruptive technologies in 1997,[9] even championed the idea (writing with Maxwell Wessel) that a company has an "extendable core" of customers who will remain even after a disrupter enters the market.[10] While Christensen's "core" is not directly related to a company's positioning, understanding it certainly enhances and elevates the value of strategic positioning.

What Do Marketers Need From Strategy?

Marketers need a cohesive strategy unifying the aims of the organization, its business plan, and its voice. Its differentiators and its competitors. Its positioning. Its hedgehog concept (to use Collins' phrase). Its reason to exist.

To paraphrase Michael Porter, marketers need a clear understanding of how the company creates competitive advantage. And, for a product, how that particular offering advances or supports the company's competitive advantage.

It states as clearly as possible how the company is going to provide value to its customers, and why that is different from the other possible options customers have at their disposal. Your strategic positioning should answer the most important questions: Who do your customers

---

[9] C. Christensen. 1997. *The Innovator's Dilemma: The Revolutionary Bestseller That Changed the Way We Do Business*. New York, NY: HarperCollins Publishers Inc.; M.E. Raynor and R. McDonald. 2015. "What Is Disruptive Innovation?" *Harvard Business Review*, pp. 44–53.

[10] M. Wessel and C.M. Christensen. 2012. "Surviving Disruption," *HBR's 10 Must Reads on Strategy, Vol. 2 (with bonus article "Creating Shared Value" By Michael E. Porter and Mark R. Kramer)*, 92. Boston: Harvard Business Review Press. Kindle Edition).

think you are? And what about your stockholders? Your employees? Your allies and suppliers? Your salespeople? They had all better be the same.

I can almost hear some of my colleagues or former clients asking if marketing shouldn't get a free pass. The answer is not just "no." It is "*emphatically*, no." Marketers need to understand that strategy is more important than design and aesthetics. More important than Instagram or Facebook. From a marketing perspective, those tools exist to support strategy. Period. And the role of creative efforts is to articulate and implement the strategy in communications at all levels.

If your great idea doesn't work with and even enhance (or, better yet, illuminate) the corporate strategy, it goes. It's really that simple.

Marketing Begins With Positioning

Marketing begins with your business strategy's positioning because marketing is a waste of time without it. If the two are not aligned, marketing may well be writing a check the business can't cash. Or making a promise the organization can't keep.

Why does strategy have to be considered at all levels? Quite simply, great corporate or business strategies can and do fall apart at the implementation stage, whether it's with marketing and branding or engineering and R&D.

Failing to clearly chart your course means you don't know where you're going or how you're going to get there. Even what you're going to do when you get there. And every direction is equally promising (or daunting).

To adapt the well-known native American proverb, your company has a good wolf and a bad wolf (at least one). The one that grows is the one you feed. If you're feeding the nonstrategic fire drills that pass for marketing at all too many corporations, you're feeding the chaos. And if you're not building your strategy, your differentiation withers and dies.

Strategic positioning can and does need to change with the times. But only with great care. And there is a cost.

A Positioning Model

As outlined previously, there are many different approaches to business strategy and positioning. Applied properly, most produce strategic direction that is clear, differentiating and actionable. As a result, strategic positioning developed with any of those models will work with the *Brand Vision* approach.

For the sake of simplicity, I have adopted the Treacy–Wiersma model throughout this text because it is extremely straightforward and clear. It helps make positioning easily understood throughout a company— who can't grasp product leadership, customer affinity, and operational excellence? And it lends itself well to a graphic approach, as shown in Figure 1.1, with the value disciplines occupying the three points of the positioning pyramid.

Several years ago, I was working with a client in the industrial equipment market, and we were trying to refine the corporate positioning. Over several hours, a team of high-level managers debated about whether the company and its products were "reliable," "high-performance," "high quality," "the industry standard," "durable," or any number of other alternatives.

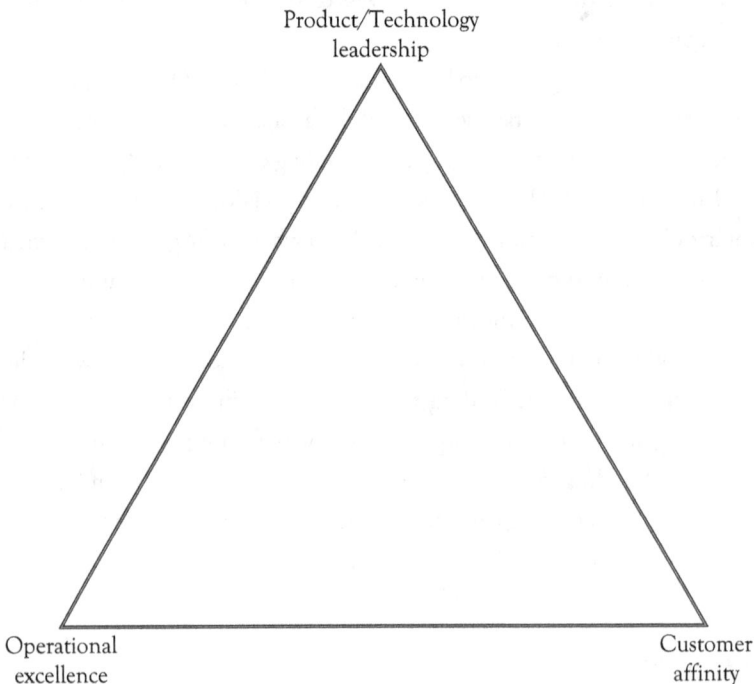

Product/Technology
leadership

Operational
excellence

Customer
affinity

Figure 1.1 The Treacy–Wiersma model, with the three value disciplines

As we later understood it, the group and the company were sales-driven. That's an excellent perspective, for sure. An absolutely vital part of the process. But it also tended to be highly idiosyncratic: Many of the players were thinking and talking anecdotally. Thinking of their interactions with a small group of customers. In some cases, no more than a handful.

After several valiant attempts, we listed all the possibilities on a whiteboard, then went around the room and asked each person to cast their vote for one of the choices. There were 12 people voting and when we tallied up the responses, 12 different "positioning statements" were selected. We knew it was time to pack it in for the day.

When we regrouped back at the agency, I realized that we were coming at things the wrong way. In essence, the team of corporate leaders, mostly engineers, were slogan-building. Somehow, we had ventured from a corporate strategy discussion into the realm of semantics. Creative phrasing, if you will. And that's not a good place to be with a dozen engineers.

I began compiling the list of terms that they used and plotting them on a white board. It looked like Figure 1.2.

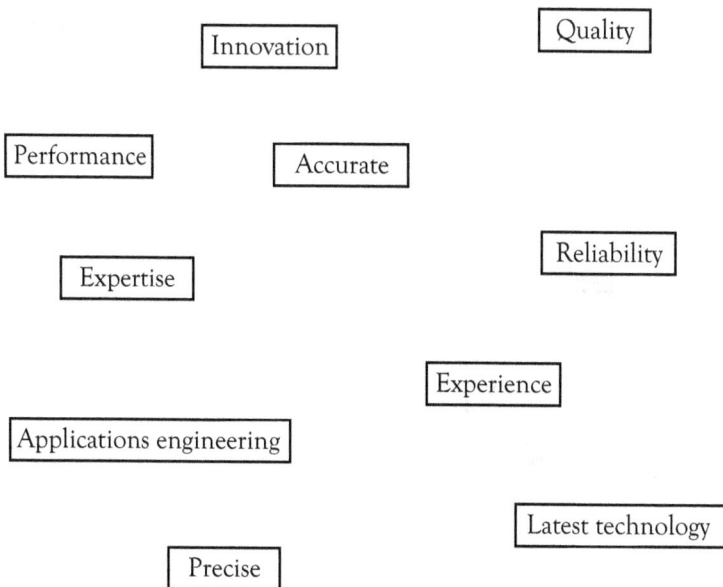

Innovation   Quality

Performance   Accurate

Expertise   Reliability

Experience

Applications engineering

Latest technology

Precise

Figure 1.2 Were the client's proposed positioning statements all over the block, as this graphic implies?

But I realized that the terms they were using were not all over the block, as they seemed. I applied this information to the Treacy–Wiersma model, then recognized that virtually all of them were product-oriented positions—terms you would use to describe a technology leader. So, rather than the jumbled mess as shown in Figure 1.3, we actually had something more like the more organized arrangement shown in Figure 1.4.

And we had our positioning answer: This company was a product/technology leadership company. And once we all agreed on that, the rest was a matter of messaging and creative wordsmithing. And that proved to be the advantage of using the Treacy–Wiersma model.

Splitting a Positioning

One interesting wrinkle occurred with two different clients, both of whom had highly engineered products that required configuration in the specific application.

Both considered application engineering an important part of their positioning, reasoning quite rightly that the expert programming of the product in the field delivered a level of performance competitors could

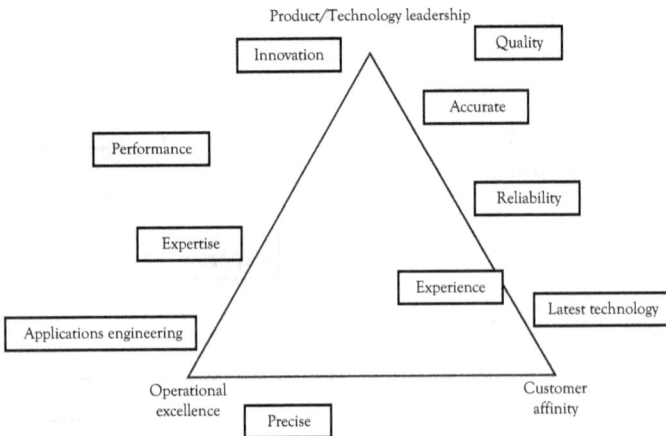

Figure 1.3 Or could the Positioning Pyramid help?

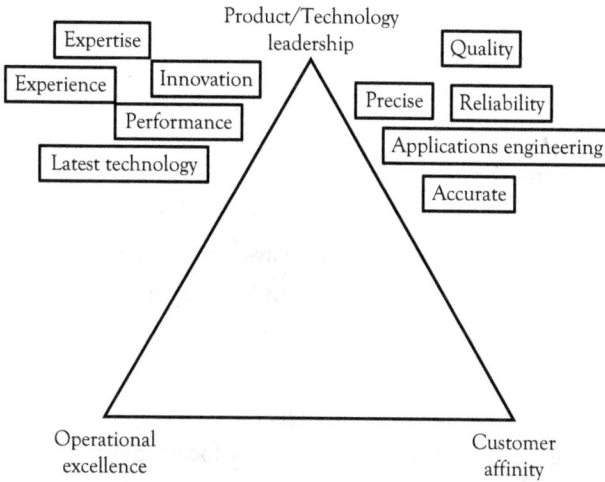

Figure 1.4 *The responses were more organized than they seemed*

never match. As a result, the configured product provided the customer with sustainable competitive advantage.

Unfortunately, both also wanted to wrap themselves in the mantle of product leadership. And, in both cases, it was well earned.

But trying to straddle both a product leadership positioning and a customer affinity positioning like application engineering expertise has its problems. Admittedly, they can be complementary. But most likely, attempting to occupy both positions means you probably won't do either well. And does the need for in-field application engineering somehow detract from the image of a high-performing, innovative product?

More importantly, where will you focus your investment for the next generation of products? On the R&D needed to create the next innovation? Or on putting more application engineers in the field, since there never seemed to be enough?

In both cases, a solution eventually presented itself because of the way the services were delivered. Both companies worked with distributors or manufacturers' representatives who were more regionally focused and had the feet on the street. It was a necessity: Neither manufacturer had enough skilled engineers or the geographic scope to be able to provide the service at customer locations. So while the core applications expertise always resided with the manufacturer, the company relied on the distributors and reps to perform the lion's share of the configuration in the field.

The compromise both companies arrived at was that they focused on cultivating their reputation as a product and technology leader. And left their distributors and reps position themselves as the skilled application experts. The arrangement was a win–win for everyone.

The main benefit of this positioning exercise is that:

- It reduces the choices at the strategic level. Instead of pondering over 30 choices (or 300), we're focusing people on three (product leadership, operational excellence, or customer affinity).
- It gets the executives and engineers focused on the core strategy, where their perspective is critical. And not on semantics or creative wordsmithing, where they are not as strong.

This positioning exercise is a good reminder of how close the product performance terms are in the broad scheme of things. The main point is that they don't have to line up perfectly. The important thing is that the terms people use to describe your company are grouped consistently around one spot—hopefully, one of the value discipline shown at the corners of the positioning pyramid. For instance, a positioning related to customer service or aftermarket support would fall under customer affinity. And price, delivery, or single-source convenience would fall under Operational Excellence.

Your goal is to develop a positioning that clearly expresses your company's essence. Approaching your business in a way that generates growth and profit, through up and down economies, undulating business cycles, changes in customer-facing personnel. And approaching your marketplace in a way your company and your employees can feel good about and accept.

Chapter Summary

Points to Remember

- Strategic positioning is the central dynamic for marketing.
- The sources of your positioning are your "crown jewels."
- Marketing needs clear positioning.

Advancing Brand Vision

Positioning gives you an elevated perspective, a commanding vantage point that resonates across the marketing process, imprinting your business strategy on everything from your creative concepts to your implementation of marketing tactics.

Next, we see how to integrate business objectives into the mix.

CHAPTER 2

Business Objectives

Chapter Overview

Many companies create business objectives as part of their annual plans or regular strategic planning. It's essential that these goals flow naturally out of the overall business strategy. And it's critical that marketers remember that tactics such as social media, PR, and e-mail are not strategies themselves. But need to fall under the high-level business strategy.

Blindsided by Business Objectives

An account manager came to me with a dilemma. The client wanted us to show how the company's marketing plan supported its business objectives developed by the company's board of directors. That was certainly a logical request, but it presented a few problems.

First, we had helped formulate the marketing plan, working with the company's marketing director. During that collaboration, no one had mentioned the business objectives. Or even that there were any. So the marketing plan was largely drafted without the benefit of the guidance provided by the board. And relating the two was going to require an after-the-fact, postdated work of fiction. Like throwing a dart at the wall and painting a target around it.

Second, no one knew exactly what the business objectives meant. One point in particular, *value innovation*, stood out as being a little unclear. Did that mean that the company should emphasize development of new products and technologies, taking value as an imperative verb? Perhaps, but none of the other two-word business objectives had a verb. So they would not be of parallel construction. Or did value innovation mean experimenting with the "value" the company delivered to customers? In today's vernacular, that sounds like a euphemism for cost-cutting.

We didn't know for sure and no one wanted to ask. We found a way to weasel-word our way through. And I later learned about value innovation when I became familiar with *Blue Ocean Strategy*[1] (mentioned in Chapter 1), which defines the term as a unique value proposition directed at creating a leap in customer value that opens up the uncontested market space envisioned in its title.

The point is not to denigrate the effort expended to develop business objectives. Far from it. It's just to point out that they often suffer the same fate as other business planning exercises, gathering dust on a shelf somewhere. Or falling on deaf ears when they do get circulated to the rank and file.

Why Business Objectives?

Companies generally like to have business objectives to define an action plan for the troops to follow. These goals can change on a more frequent basis than business strategies, usually annually. They are the specific actions or plans the company is implementing to achieve and embody its business strategy. Boards of directors like them, for good reason. They see them as advancing the strategy for the company.

By developing business objectives, top executives give focus and direction to the rank and file. Perhaps even more importantly, they demonstrate management's commitment to their stated business strategy.

But there are problems occasionally. Suppose managers stray from their business strategy and take the opportunity with their objectives to enshrine the value disciplines they rejected at the strategy level? A good example would be a product leadership company deciding that "raising customer satisfaction" or "lowering costs" would be suitable business objectives.

While these points may be areas where the company wants to improve (and who doesn't want to achieve both of those), they do not further the business strategy and are not in the sweet spot for a product leadership company in the way that introducing new products or owning a technology or thought leadership position would be.

---

[1] W.C. Kim and R. Mauborgne. 2015. *Blue Ocean Strategy: How to Create Uncontested Market Space and Make the Competition Irrelevant*. Boston: Harvard Business School Publishing.

Departing from the business strategy in this way would muddy the waters, sending mixed messages to the troops. It would tell them that the business strategy was "flexible." Negotiable, even. And that their leaders were only paying lip service to the overall master plan. It would invite freelancing by line managers, implying that diverging from the business strategy would be tolerated. Perhaps even welcomed.

It thus would put a company squarely in the muddled middle that Porter warned of. Being as unstrategic as a company with no business strategy whatsoever.

So it's extremely important that a company's business objectives reflect the business strategy it has embraced. And while there can be flexibility in the specific objectives a company adopts, there are some goals that fit well with individual business strategies based on the individual value disciplines.

The Thorny Problem of Growth

Growth is a special concern for a business strategy. It's almost in everyone's list of objectives, of course. But it can be a problem, as Michael Porter notes.[2]

The trade-offs and hard choices so necessary to strategy can result in real or perceived limits on growth. By maintaining the price needed to support a customer affinity strategy or excluding a set of customers because they don't meet the strategic criteria, a company does, in fact, limit growth, perhaps in the short term.

And, as one marketing manager suggested to me, it may be *strategic* to allow "cheap and dirty" competitors to build a business by picking off the low-hanging fruit. But it might not be smart, especially when the ultimate goal of these new competitors is to improve their quality and challenge your core business in the long term.

"You can't operate with blinders on," he said.

---

[2] M.E. Porter. 1996. "What Is Strategy?" *HBR's 10 Must Reads on Strategy (including featured article "What Is Strategy?" by Michael E. Porter)*, 24. Harvard Business Review Press. Kindle Edition.

Matching Objectives to Business Strategy

A product leadership company, as noted, would be focused on introducing new products and owning a technology leadership position. A customer affinity company should always be looking at customer satisfaction and increasing its share of wallet. And a price-oriented operational excellence company would be paying attention to price and market share (see the Examples box for more detail).

Some Examples of Business Objectives (by Strategy)

Below are some obvious business objectives that match the main business strategies.

Product Leadership

- Introduce new products
- Own the technology leadership position
- Increase sales/Gain market share

Operational Excellence (Price/Delivery)

- Lower costs
- Own the low-cost position
- Increase sales/Gain market share

Operational Excellence (Quality)

- Improve quality
- Own the product quality position
- Increase sales/Gain market share (especially among quality-conscious customers)

Customer Affinity

- Improve customer satisfaction score
- Own the customization positioning
- Improve share of wallet

Measurement

Some experts encourage execs to attach metrics to these objectives. For instance, "Increase sales ten percent." That does attract a little more attention and even expresses a sense of urgency, transforming the objective from a vague wish or "nice to have" to a measurable goal.

In some companies, achievement of that goal becomes part of a manager's evaluation, determining their bonus or even their continued employment.

The Balanced Scorecard was developed as a way to move beyond purely financial considerations and create a way for a company to determine whether, in addition to meeting sales and profit goals, it is achieving its long-term strategic objectives.

There's good reason for that. As Michael C. Mankins and Richard Steele wrote in "Turning Great Strategy into Great Performance," companies that closely integrate strategy, planning, and performance experience a "multiplier effect"[3] in long-term business success.

Marketing Strategies and Objectives

Many companies develop marketing strategies and objectives as well as business strategies and objectives. As noted earlier, I am reluctant to create a separate marketing strategy. Marketing strategy is the business strategy. Period.

Here's why: There shouldn't be a marketing strategy any more than there should be a PR, e-mail, or social media strategy. The temptation to go rogue is simply too great. And I haven't found many marketing directors who were successful at resisting it.

I get it that all these functions want to be strategic. That's a good thing. So I developed another model, the strategic marketing pyramid, to show how marketing initiatives connect to the business strategy and objectives, as illustrated in Figure 2.1.

---

[3] M.C. Mankins and R. Steele. 2005. "Turning Great Strategy into Great Performance," *HBR's 10 Must Reads on Strategy (including featured article "What Is Strategy?" by Michael E. Porter)*, 150. Boston: Harvard Business Review Press. Kindle Edition.

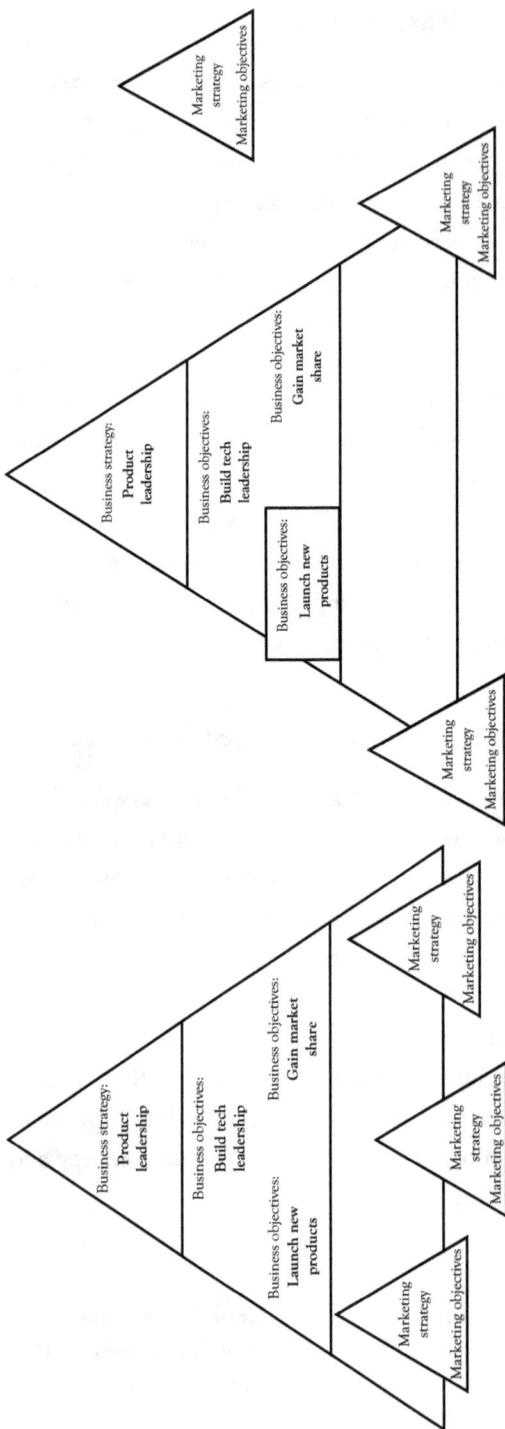

Figure 2.1 *Some would have us believe that Marketing Strategies and Objectives can live under the business strategy and business objective, as shown on the left. But that approach all too often gives marketers a license to create renegade strategies not really attached to the business strategy and objectives. And what most often happens is shown on the right*

If you want to develop a separate marketing strategy, by all means do so. But remember the cautionary tale mentioned previously. And make sure the marketing strategies relate to and even amplify the business strategy.

Can social media, e-mail, PR, or other tactics be strategic by connecting *on their own* to business strategy and business objectives? The short answer is no. It's not strategic to have these initiatives operating separately, as if the others don't exist. Not strategic. Not effective. Certainly not cost efficient. Why? Because these tactics work so much better when they're coordinated. Integrated. Designed to work together in a campaign to achieve business objectives (more on this in Chapter 7).

There can be some additional marketing objectives, of course, but usually only in furtherance of business objectives. For example, adding distributors is an obvious marketing objective but absolutely must come directly out of the business objectives. And if a marketing initiative does not support the business strategy and business objectives, you probably shouldn't be doing it.

Otherwise, you run the risk of a rogue operation, which is the real danger of having marketing strategies and objectives. It's the real temptation and the start of the "social media strategies" debacle that is a constant pressure.

It's better to have some business objectives that obviously are designed to implement and further the business strategy (as shown in Figure 2.2). Then all marketing initiatives connect to the business objectives and every marketing initiative supports the business strategy and at least one business objective (as shown in Figure 2.3) and maybe more (Figure 2.4).

It's important to note that marketing does not meet those business objectives on its own. Only by working in concert with other functions, such as sales, engineering, or R&D, does it meet these objectives.

When you're looking at overall marketing program and all the marketing initiatives, it had better make sense that you are doing specific initiatives to support an objective. It ought to seem as if the marketing initiative was crafted specifically to help the company meet that objective.

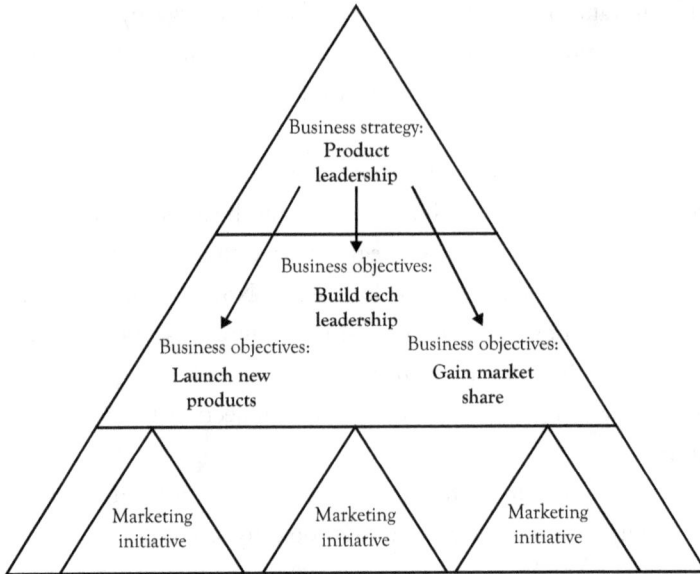

Figure 2.2 *The best approach is to make sure business objectives truly support the business strategy*

Figure 2.3 *And, in turn, the various marketing initiatives support the business objectives*

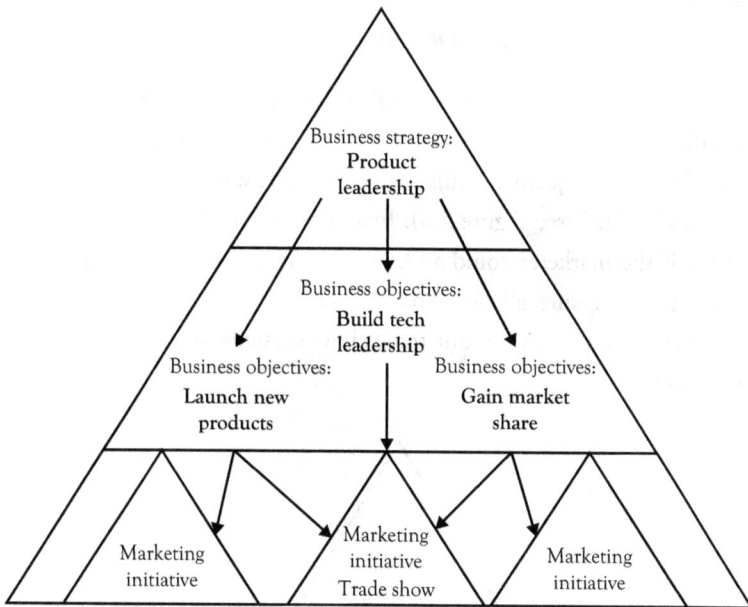

Figure 2.4 It's easy to see how a specific marketing initiative (e.g., trade show) might support more than one objective (increase sales/ share, own leadership position, etc.)

And when you look at all the initiatives supporting a business objective, they ought to look like a concerted, complete effort to achieve the objective. With all the departments and disciplines in a company harnessed and working cooperatively to achieve that objective.

That avoids the problem mentioned in the introduction to this chapter, where various functions (like marketing) are trying to retrofit their pet projects into the company's business objectives. Using them as window-dressing and not really making an effort to achieve that goal specifically. Certainly not *designed* to achieve that objective.

In fact, if companies really want to achieve their business objectives, they may want to consider assembling a team of senior executives and empower them with the cross-department authority to develop a program to meet those goals.

Strategy Travels in Both Directions

Business objectives and marketing initiatives ought to be mutually reinforcing. With it making sense that the specific initiative is a way to achieve the objective: "This is a really smart way to build technology leadership" (see Figure 2.5). Imagine what a difference it would make if the marketer could add, "And we're working with our sales team to make sure all our reps are prepared to take advantage of the way we're promoting our trade show presence to customers and prospects."

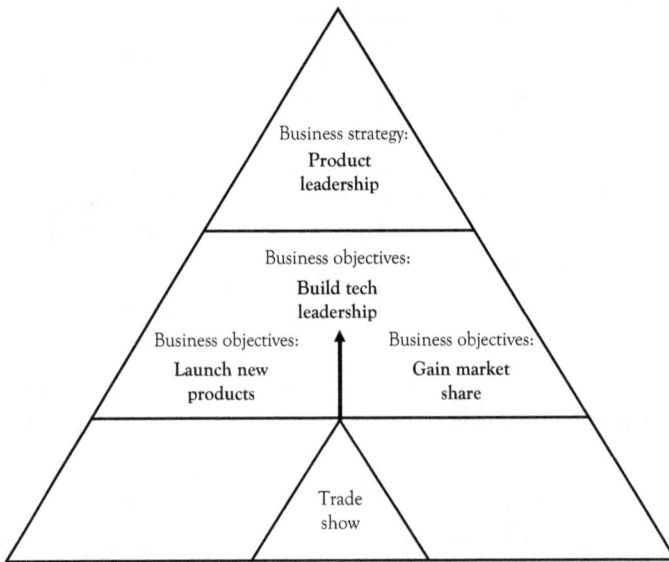

Figure 2.5 It makes sense that if marketers are proposing the idea of exhibiting at a trade show, they can support that initiative by showing how it will help the company build technology leadership

And it should work the other way: with the business objective offering compelling logic about why the specific marketing initiative needs to be approved and funded (see Figure 2.6). In essence, "There's no better way to build technology leadership than to go to the show."

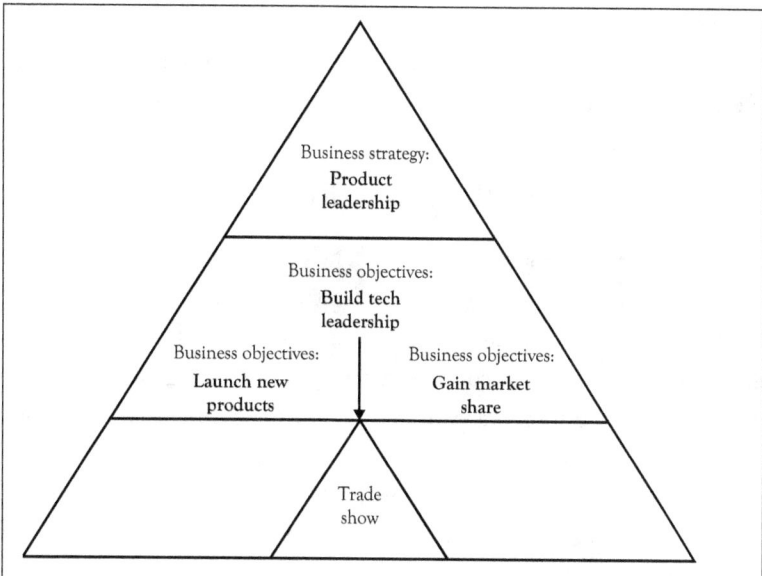

Figure 2.6 And it also makes sense that if one of your business objectives is to build technology leadership, then going to an industry show could be an important element of that plan

When you are presenting results to top management, it's always a good idea to be prepared to explain how your initiative supports the business objectives and vice versa. There's no better way to show you're thinking strategically.

The Competitive Landscape

A few years ago, a chemical company came to us with a typical issue. They were being spun off from a major conglomerate where they currently resided and would need to create a new identity in the marketplace.

There was strong sentiment inside the company to revert to one of the previous brands, which still had a high level of recognition in the marketplace. However, top management was concerned that reverting to the old name would send the wrong impression, especially since the company believed its new positioning should center on innovation.

I conducted more than 40 interviews, both with company insiders and customers around the world. The results were surprising, to say the least.

Yes, the company was seen as innovative. But so were many of its competitors. Who, by the way, were well-resourced and highly regarded. We needed to find something else (for the rest of the story, see Chapter 5).

The Benefits of Research

The previous example shows that it really helps to have some solid research to back up your positioning in a competitive market. At the very least, you'll want to interview customers and noncustomers, as well as sales and distribution partners. You could do a survey, but you won't have the ability to probe in depth the way you would with a one-on-one conversation.

The goal is to go beyond limiting survey data to find out how the audience really feels about your company. You'll want to establish not just who the major players are, but who is the technology leader? Who leads in operational excellence, both in price and in quality? Who stands out in customer affinity, especially in customizing products and services unique to each customer?

The Brand Landscape Pyramid

I adapted the positioning pyramid from Chapter 1 into a Brand Landscape Pyramid (Figure 2.7) to help make it easier to visualize how the competitive troops are arrayed across the marketing "battlefield." It uses the value disciplines as the points of the pyramid.

Doing this exercise helps you know where competitors are positioning themselves and what places on the competitive landscape are contested. And what might be available.

Creating the Competitive Landscape Pyramid

Start by reviewing your audience research. Then look at the existing marketing of the major competitors, including their paid placements, websites, and social media pages. These materials help you learn how your competitors are presenting themselves to the world. The more sophisticated they are, the more their messages will be consistent and aligned with one of the three main business strategies. You may, of course, find

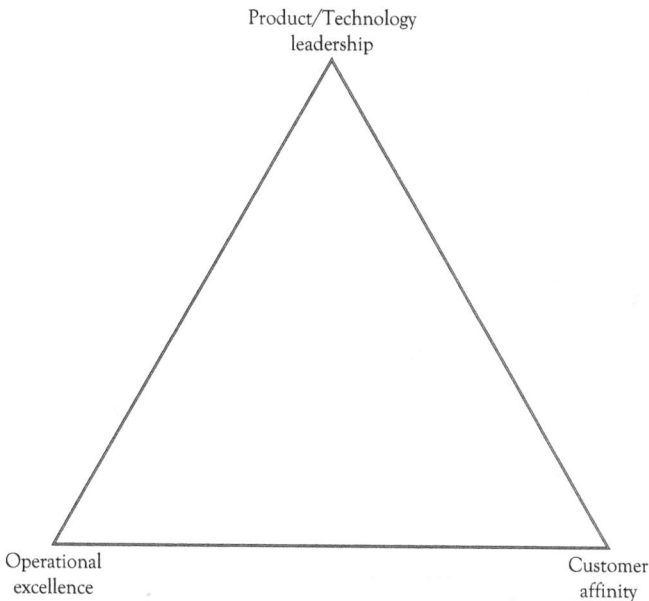

Figure 2.7 The brand landscape pyramid

some competitors who are all over the block, trying to be all things to all customers. But that is becoming more and more rare.

And remember that a competitor's marketing may not accurately reflect how they are perceived in the marketplace. So you will want to be comparing the feedback you get from your research with the messaging that lives on a company's website and marketing materials.

Once you have those key positions determined, you'll want to plot them on the competitive landscape pyramid accordingly.

Start with the main competitor, affixing their logo in the position that best suits them (Figure 2.8).

Next add in the other competitors (see Figure 2.9). Feel free to straddle a position if their marketing and your research indicates that's what's happening. But remember, as noted in Chapter 1, that's not something *you* want to do. Straddling two (or more) strategic points as Competitors B and C are doing, shows weakness, not strength. Most companies can hardly afford to occupy one spot, let alone two.

Finally, place your company where it is currently (see Figure 2.10).

Product/Technology
leadership

Competitor A

Operational   Customer
excellence   affinity

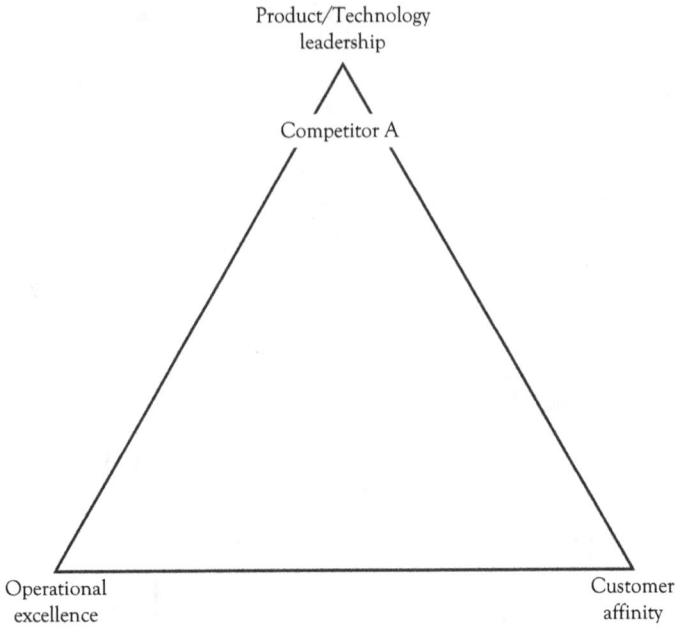

Figure 2.8 Place the first competitor in the position that fits them
the best

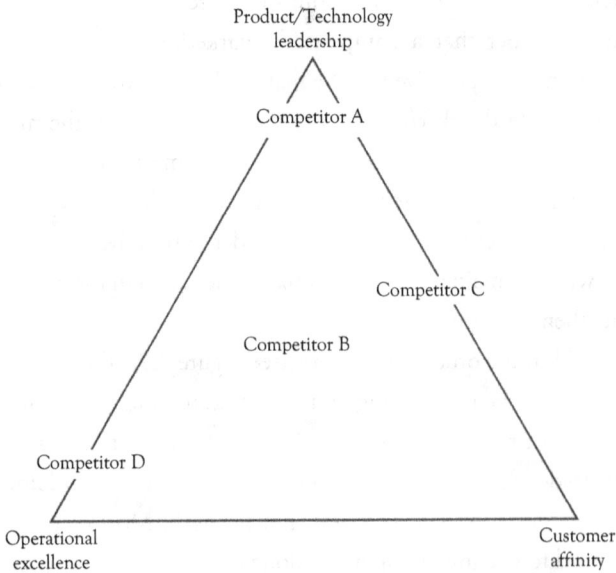

Product/Technology
leadership

Competitor A

Competitor C

Competitor B

Competitor D

Operational   Customer
excellence   affinity

Figure 2.9 Place all the competitors in the most appropriate position

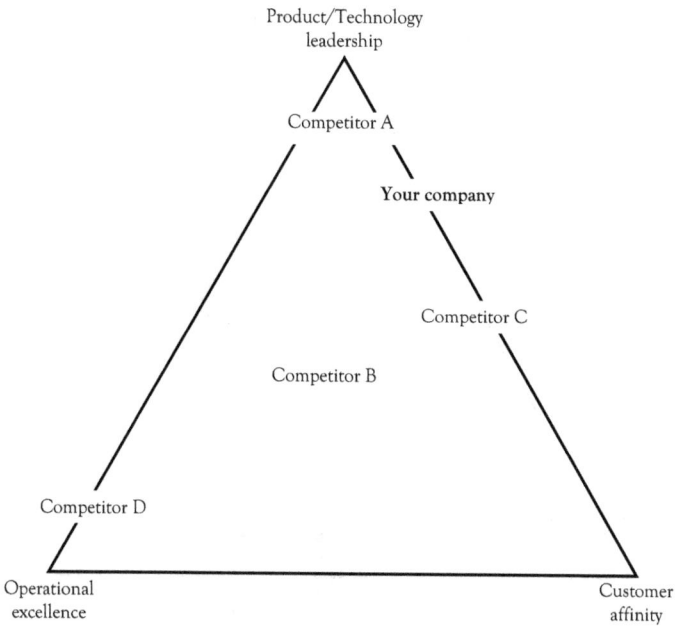

Figure 2.10 *Place your company in its position*

Then survey the landscape. Have you placed your company where it really is in the competitive landscape? And are there any spots that are more appropriate ... and open? Especially, any worth having?

Let me stress that a competitor's presence should not necessarily deter you from taking a position. It's important to recognize, however, that a well-funded, entrenched competitor is difficult to dislodge, especially if they have a strong identity. If you have a better claim to the spot than they do, go for it. But know that's what you're getting into and understand that you'll need to marshal greater resources.

In our current example, could you occupy the Customer Affinity position, based on what you found in your research (Figure 2.11)? And should you consider that?

The answer, of course, is that marketers can't do that unilaterally. Changing positions on this pyramid goes right to the heart of the business strategy. But this is a useful tool that top management may want to consider in examining or renewing business strategy. Especially in a crowded field, where there is a lot of red ocean competition.

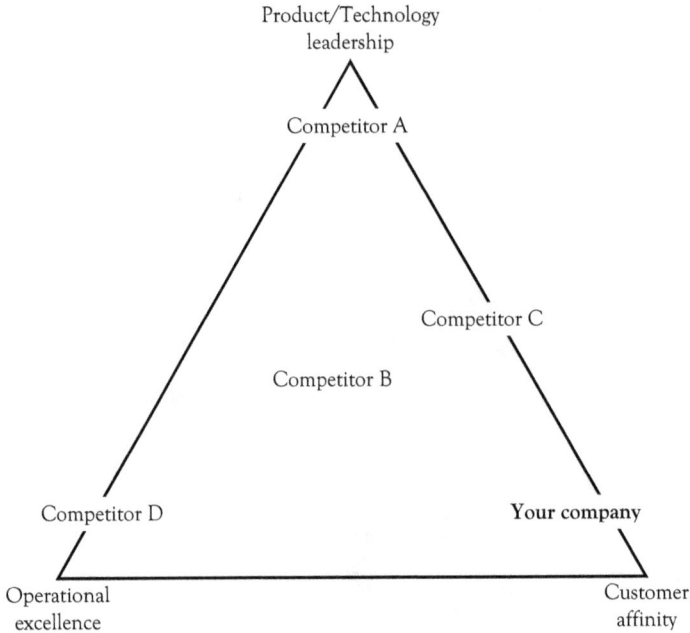

Figure 2.11 Would it be appropriate to consider an alternative positioning?

Specialized "Poles"

You can change the locations in the pyramid for circumstances unique to the industry. In industrial chemicals, for instance, sustainability or a "green" reputation is important. In others, safety can be important. Meanwhile, in industries that are highly regulated, like banking, product leadership may not be an issue.

Brand Preference

As part of the postmerger integration (PMI) efforts of two global corporations, our client wanted to demonstrate that its marketing and promotion were not only registering increases in brand recognition but also were achieving improvements in preference.

Preference, of course, is the next best thing to sales. If you're the brand preferred by the majority of the market, sales generally will follow. But it doesn't happen overnight.

The campaign we had run was closely tied to the three key tenets of the messaging strategy (see Chapter 2).

Now the client was asking us to conduct research to determine not only the success of the marketing effort, but of the company as well. As measured by the preference for the brand.

For good reason. It is much easier to change a marketing campaign than it is to change a company. And many, of course, have launched a media blitz with little regard for the realities out there in the field. One case where a company succeeded in changing its market perception via an advertising campaign is Ford's "Quality is Job One" campaign.

The Campaign

We were able to convince our client that its PMI campaign was an opportunity to do more than simply introduce the new brand. We convinced them to make the PMI announcement about the important values that supported the positioning of the new brand.

We believed that it's the height of marketing arrogance to believe that customers really care about new names and logos. But we make them care—even excite them—by talking about the new capabilities the merged company will offer. And the ways in which it would help the audience of design engineers build competitive advantage into their products.

The goal was not to have customers see the logo and think it was cool. Rather, it was to see the branding as an avatar for the product quality and technology leadership the company had to offer.

Building Brand Preference

Entire books have been written about developing preference for a brand, well beyond the scope of this inquiry. The key points:

- A brand needs to be more than a logo and graphics. It's the sum total of all the things the audience believes about your company.

- Customers have to care about the value benefits you're promoting. These values have to connect with them.
- The values have to be true. It's a lot easier to promote something that's real.

It's crazy to try to build brand preference if those points aren't true.

The Results

For our client, the disciplined campaign was a major success in every regard. The deciding research for our client was a survey of several thousand members of the audience, asking them to state their awareness of and preference for the company and its key competitors. Then compare them on several key parameters, using a five-point scale.

First, the new brand achieved a level of recognition that not only exceeded the awareness of either of the previous brands but also surpassed the brand recognition of the two companies *combined*.

And secondly, the level of preference on key performance parameters was also a success. We graphically portrayed those result, taking our cue from the competitive landscape pyramid mentioned before (see Figure 2.12).

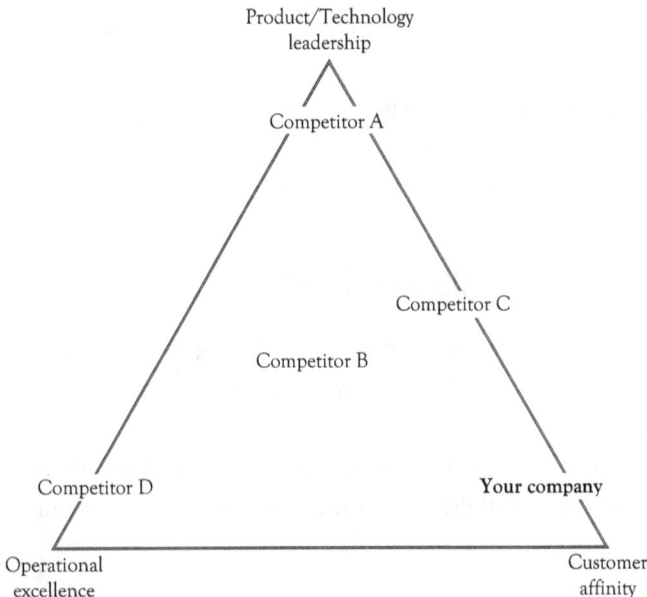

Figure 2.12 The competitive landscape pyramid

We then took the data from the brand preference study and created a scale radiating out from the center of the pyramid (Figure 2.13). To make the differences more apparent, we made the center a 3.0 average, since none of the major competitors scored below 3.0 on any of the criteria.

We compared the results year after year and saw the growth in the client's brand preference over several years. The approach helped us document progress from year to year and know whether our marketing was moving the brand needle (or not).

In this case, our B2B client made clear progress, year after year, in becoming the preferred product leadership brand in the category. And increasing sales and market share as a result.

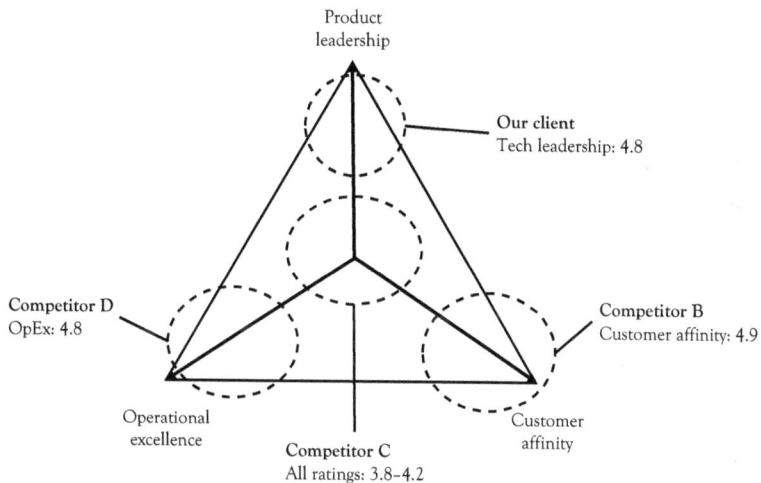

Figure 2.13 *Translating preference data onto the brand landscape*

Alternatives to Branding Studies

Unfortunately, doing brand preference studies is expensive, usually costing more than most companies can afford on a regular basis. There are other alternatives, though not as definitive perhaps. The Net Promoter Score (NPS) advanced by Frederick F. Reichheld[4] has proven to be an

---

[4] F.F. Reichheld. 2003. "The One Number You Need to Grow," *HBR's 10 Must Reads on Strategic Marketing (with featured article "Marketing Myopia," by Theodore Levitt)*, 151–169. Boston: Harvard Business Review Press. Kindle Edition.

effective measure of a brand's likely success. And I have also used web analytics tools like page visits as an informal indicator and a great tool to optimize a campaign (more on this in Chapter 9).

Chapter Summary

Points to Remember

- Business objectives should flow out of the strategy.
- Tactics such as social media, PR, and e-mail are not strategies.
- A brand needs to be more than a logo and graphics.

Advancing Brand Vision

Nothing excites top executives quite as much as laying out the competitive landscape like a battlefield. The exercise usually sparks high-level discussions about where your company is and where it's going. That information gives direction that can inform and guide marketing tactics.

Next, we start talking about the market forces that shape the competitive landscape in which you'll be operating.

PART II

Audience: Intelligence That Resonates

It's important to know who you are talking to. Is it average consumers? Kids? Engineers? Parents? School administrators? Maintenance departments?

And what are the audience's concerns? Cost? Quality? Performance? Energy use? Safety? Regulatory compliance?

That's the only way you'll know how to address them and their concerns specifically.

But that's easier said than done. The issues are many.

The buying team is growing, adding new players and new perspectives.

New roles are being included, like Human Relations (HR); Environmental Health and Safety (EHS); Information Technology (IT); Maintenance, Repair, and Operations (MRO), to name a few.

Market dynamics are constantly changing, as new entrants enter an already crowded field. Industries and competitors are becoming truly global. And rules, organizing principles, and terminology vary from industry to industry.

To succeed in this rapidly changing environment, marketers need new understanding and new tools to handle all these new concerns. They need to recognize that a benefit like rugged reliability might matter to an end user. But to a distributor or original equipment manufacturer (OEM), not so much.

And the information an IT manager needs is much different than the data you need to provide an HR manager or product designer.

CHAPTER 3

The Market

Chapter Overview

Defining how your company fits into the industry landscape is a crucial step in developing effective marketing communications. Equally important is knowing your customer's place in that industry structure. As we will see, the same product may have different benefits to individual customers.

Industry Structure

You would think that most companies know what industry they're selling into. And, of course, most do, especially if they're selling to consumers.

Except that some companies sell into more than one industry. In fact, some have dozens, if not hundreds, of industrial applications. And some, because they sell through distribution, don't really know exactly where or even how their products are used. As a result, it's always a good idea to specify what industry you're selling into.

However, even that isn't enough for marketing purposes. Most industries have a structure, a way of doing business, with a variety of different companies playing different roles. Understanding how your company—and your target customers—fit into that industry landscape is critical. It's the essence of B2B marketing and it's critical to the development of creative content and messaging.

As we'll see here, it's absolutely essential to know who you're selling to. The same product will pay different benefits to different people, with one influencer concerned about a product's quality, a second person wanting to know how easy it is to use, and yet a third caring only about price. It all depends on a prospect's role in the process.

A few major types of industry organization are described in the following. Please note that the list is intended to be illustrative and not exhaustive. There are experts who have spent their entire careers mapping industry organization and this work is not intended to replace or even summarize their efforts. The goal here is simply to expose readers to the diversity of the industrial landscape.

These structures are growing, changing, and morphing on almost a daily basis, so these examples are just a snapshot of what is going on at any one moment. The relationships vary tremendously from industry to industry. And some, like the automotive industry, actually exhibit all the models mentioned here.

The Direct Model

We can start with the simplest model, where companies sell directly to their customers (Figure 3.1). This is basically the retail model, with stores, brick-and-mortar or virtual, selling directly to consumers. And while this is common, it is by no means the norm in business today.

But while this model may seem commonplace, actually it isn't. Most major industries, from food processors to car companies, do not sell direct to consumers. They sell through distribution systems.

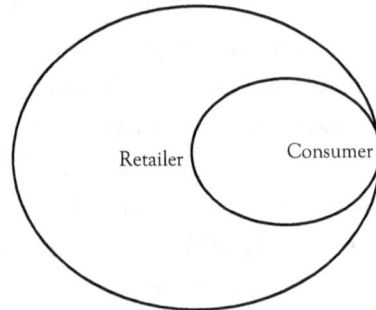

Figure 3.1 The direct model

The Distribution Model

Many industrial products are sold through distribution systems as shown in Figure 3.2. Cars, for instance, are sold through dealers (although selling direct is starting to emerge).

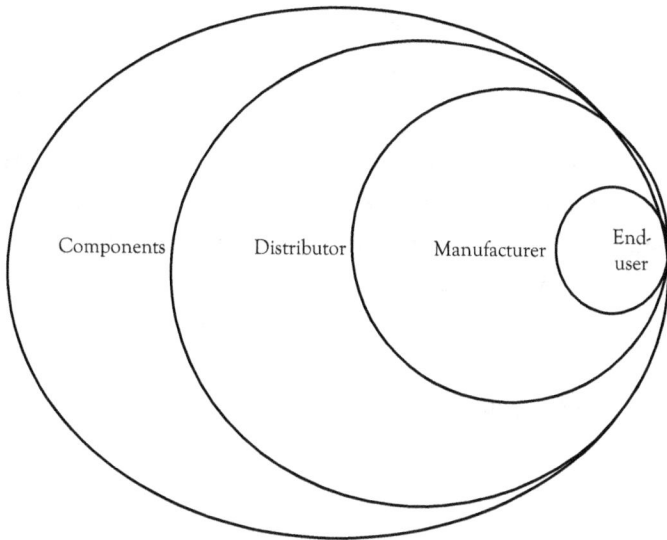

Figure 3.2 Distributors want to own the relationship with the end user

Industrial distributors play an important role in the sale of industrial products for a number of reasons. They offer convenience, inventory, and some expertise in product selection, to name just a few things. Some distributors have exclusive relationships with their manufacturers, meaning they sell no other products, or at least none that compete directly. Others do not. The deciding factor is the strength of the manufacturer's brand: The stronger the brand, the more clout they have in negotiating a demand for exclusivity.

Dealers are a special type of distribution method, because they are much more brand loyal, meaning they are much more tied to the manufacturer's brand. The best examples are car dealers. Most try to establish their own identify, but few achieve enough marketing clout to rival that of the car companies, even in their local markets. Car makers, with their huge investments in marketing, have most of the clout. It's easy to see why. What do you do if your local dealership stops carrying Fords? Where do you go for authorized service? And will you switch to one of the dealership's Toyotas or Hondas when you are ready to replace your trusty vehicle, especially if you love that brand?

Manufacturer's Representatives

Independent manufacturer's representatives are another category of distribution with individual sales operations that usually don't have warehouses and stock products. But, once again, they build that all-important relationship with the customer. Most reps do not have exclusive relationships with one manufacturer, generally handling multiple lines, some of which may even compete. A classic example occurs in the commercial lighting industry, where independent reps often sell lighting products from a major manufacturer like Philips, as well as specialty lighting from dozens of smaller companies.

Tiered Structures

The vast army of suppliers who service the automotive market are organized in a tiered structure, with a handful of car makers like Ford and General Motors designated as Tier One OEMs. As noted previously, they sell to consumers like you and me through their networks of dealers.

But in addition to this admittedly large consumer market, there are literally tens of thousands of companies that manufacture the parts and services the large auto makers purchase to assemble their vehicles. And not all of them are small. The list includes billion-dollar multinational companies, like Magna, Lear, and Robert Bosch.

Here's how the structure works. Let's start with a consumer like you and me who wants to buy a car (Figure 3.3).

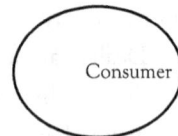

Figure 3.3 To build a tiered industry structure, we start with the consumer—the car buyer in the automotive industry

We buy that car from one of the car companies, such as Ford, Toyota, General Motors, or Honda (as shown in Figure 3.4). In the industry, they are known as original equipment manufacturers, or OEMs.

Next, a (relatively) small group of Tier Two suppliers (shown in Figure 3.5) make modules and systems—think major system elements

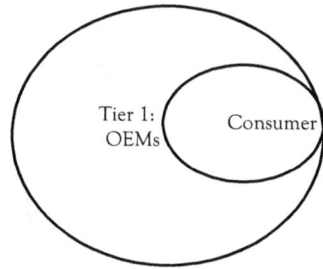

Figure 3.4 Then we add the car company, the original equipment manufacturer (OEM)

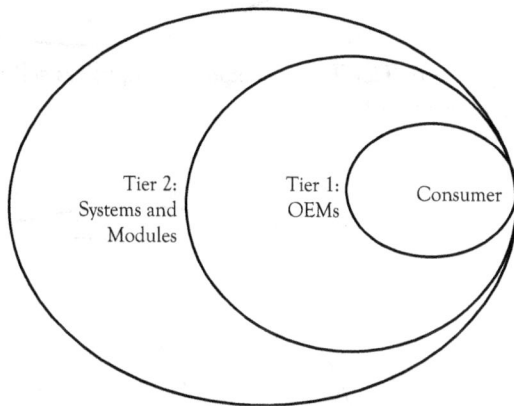

Figure 3.5 Tier Two manufacturers sell directly to the car companies, the OEMs

such as interior trim or the chassis—that are sold to the OEMs. For example, Tier Two manufacturers like Faurecia, Johnson Controls, or Lear sell entire seat assemblies to the large automotive companies.

Another group of Tier Three component suppliers, shown in Figure 3.6, sells to these Tier Two module/systems companies. In this case, a Tier Three manufacturer might sell a seat suspension component system to one of the Tier Two manufacturers like Johnson Controls.

And finally, those Tier Three component makers, in turn, buy parts from the Tier Four companies (as shown in Figure 3.7). The example here might be a manufacturer of foam, leather, or springs, sold to the Tier Three component company.

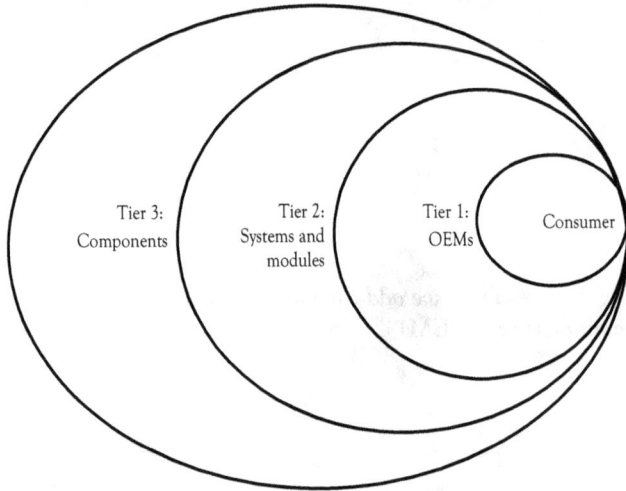

Figure 3.6 Tier Three component suppliers sell to the Tier Two Systems manufacturers

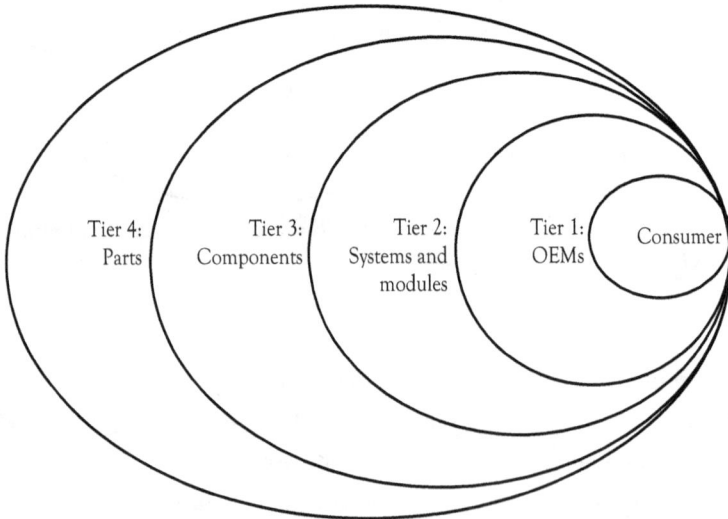

Figure 3.7 The automotive market has a tiered structure, with the major car makers like Ford and General Motors identified as Tier 1 original equipment manufacturers (OEMs)

Other industries like computers have tiered structures as well. Most computer companies, for instance, do not make their own computer chips and may not even do the circuit boards. So they have thousands of suppliers producing mother boards, connectors, and even chips. The 21st century version of cottage industries, if you will.

The tiered structures help keep the large manufacturers from being inundated by the thousands of suppliers who already sell components, parts, and systems into the industry. The tier structure forces suppliers to stay in their lanes and not try to jump ahead to the next highest tier.

Competitive Advantage

Throughout this process, the various players are looking to establish competitive advantage. What can they do that makes them unique or absolutely indispensable to their customers?

Manufacturers of parts, components, systems, and assemblies are always looking to improve the quality, performance, and reliability of their products. They're hoping that these upgrades will provide competitive advantage over their competitors. Creating the perception of value further up the line is important for companies who hope to command a premium price. Intel, of course, is the best example, with a famous campaign in the 1990s that had consumers looking for the "Intel Inside" sticker when they went to buy a computer.

The key is getting customers to recognize a component brand and be willing to pay more for it. It's all about differentiation. Giving them the perception that the product without the branded component simply wouldn't measure up. And making the presence of the component a deciding factor in the sale, as Intel did in the critical stage of the electronics revolution where compatibility between systems was a crucial factor.

It's also why the automotive OEMs keep the design and manufacture of key components—especially engines—in house. Their differentiation is at stake.

There's a problem, however, when a supplier of a critical component or system becomes too dominant. For example, Rockwell's Allen Bradley ControlLogix control system became so pervasive in North America at one point that it was difficult for their customers—manufacturers of industrial equipment like Computer Numerical Control (CNC) machining centers—to offer a lot of differentiation. After all, these machine makers were all using the same control system, so how different could they be? That made it attractive for suppliers of competitive control systems—especially European suppliers—to gain a foothold in the market.

Similarly, distributors jealously guard their relationships with their customers, feeling quite rightly that their suppliers could cut them out of the relationship and go direct. There is ample precedent for that fear, as is illustrated in another Rockwell example, where the company struggled to find ways to handle the needs of high-volume maintenance and repair customers.[1] There is also a lot of channel conflict around geographic territories, as growing dealers vie for distributor status (and pricing).[2]

During the initial run-up to e-commerce, I was involved in several dustups when manufacturers took tentative steps toward direct selling online. And they had to shut down these efforts because their distributor customers complained bitterly.

That's why distributors are always looking for a way to add value that their industrial customer will care about. For some, that value might include application engineering expertise, with distributors assisting their customers in finding the right product for their particular needs. Or even working with a manufacturer to configure a product that meets a customer's specifications or designing the system in which the component will function.

Why Market Structure Matters

These distinctions are important to marketing because your customer's place in the industry structure strongly influences the importance of certain benefits such as product price, quality, or durability. It determines whether it matters (or not) that your company has the ability to customize a product to meet a manufacturer's specific needs.

---

[1] M. Sawhney, M. Biddlecom, R. Day, P. Franke, J. Lee-Tin, R. Leonard, and B. Poger. 2004. *Rockwell Automation: The Channel Challenge.* Kellogg School of Management. https://hbsp.harvard.edu/product/KEL163-PDF-ENG?Ntt=marketing%20through%20distributors

[2] M. Taylor and M. Vandenbosch. 2012. "Bolter Electronics: Dealing with Dealer Demands," *Ivey Publishing.* https://hbsp.harvard.edu/product/W12242-PDF-ENG

Distributors, for instance, probably aren't terribly concerned about product longevity, because a failure 5 or 10 years down the road isn't an issue for them. It may even be a potential selling opportunity.

Similarly, a systems supplier may not be interested in customization, if the part is largely a commodity. Price may be the only thing that interests them.

So the same product could well be sold differently, depending on who you are talking to. Because what they care about may be different.

What Matters

Our client came to us with an unusual request. For a global meeting of its board of directors, the company wanted us to explain the difference between two critical types of customers—distributors and OEMs.

Partly, the request was a result of the global nature of the company. The board was located in Europe, which created two important differences. First, board members were not as familiar with industrial distributors, which are less common in Europe. And second, the company's brand was well known in its home country and neighboring ones, But, in the United States, not so much.

The second point was something we dealt with frequently. In Europe, everyone wanted to be associated with the brand because of its German engineering and reputation for quality. In the United States, it was just one of a hundred brands vying for the customer's attention.

The first point, though, is an enduring challenge. Knowing the difference between talking to distributors, who resell your product and thus are more of a partner than a customer. And OEMs, who use your product and services in the machines they make. Or even the ones they use to manufacture their own products.

What Matters and What Doesn't ... to Whom

Understanding the benefits that are relevant to the different players will go a long way toward helping you market to individual players. And while these can vary from industry to industry and company to company, they follow a few basic patterns.

A summary of the hot buttons at each level is shown in Table 3.1.

Tier One

If you're talking to a **manufacturing engineer**, they care whether your system or module will drop into their process and make their assembly line run more smoothly. They are expecting Six-Sigma quality. And they want to know if it can allow mass customization (with bar codes allowing unit customization). While many tend to believe initial price is important, these manufacturing aids can dwarf initial price in their impact on applied cost.

If you're talking to a **design engineer**, on the other hand, they'll be looking for product technologies and innovations that improve performance and thus give them a chance to build competitive advantage into their product.

Tier Two

New technical innovations are important to Tier Two, as they help their customer (the Tier One) achieve goals such as weight or size reduction or overall product performance. Quality and process compatibility are also important.

Tier Three

When the Tier Four commodity parts supplier approaches the Tier Three manufacturer, price becomes more important. Then overall quality. New materials allowing performance improvements do surface on occasion, of course. But the day-to-day grind is mostly about price and delivery.

Tier Four

Because the company at this level sells most on price, the cost of their raw materials is paramount. And, of course, controlling quality of the manufacturing input is important in helping them achieve their goals.

The Hot Buttons: A Summary

Table 3.1 The relative importance of key benefits to the various players in the process, with one being the least important and five being the most important

Tiered Structures

Role	Selling to...	Description	Fit process	Brand loyal	New technical capabilities	Quality, purity	Price	Reliability, durability	Custom
Supplier	Tier 4	Raw materials	5	1	3	5	5	1	1
Tier 4	Tier 3	Commodity parts	5	1	4	5	5	3	1
Tier 3	Tier 2	Component	5	1	5	5	3	4	5
Tier 2	Tier 1	System or module	5+	1	5	5	1	5	5

Distribution

Role	Stock product?	Exclusive	Brand loyal	New tech capabilities	Quality, purity	Price	Reliability, durability	Custom
Distributor	Yes	Somewhat	5	4	2	3	1	4
Manufacturers rep	No	Moderately	5	3	1	3	1	1
Dealer	Yes	Possibly	5	3	5	3	1	1
Original Equipment Manufacturer	No	Not at all	1	5	5	1	5	5

Chapter Summary

Points to Remember

- It's critical to understand how you fit into the industry landscape.
- Your customer's place in the industry structure affects what's important to them.
- Different benefits may be important to different types of customers.

Advancing Brand Vision

By better understanding the structure of the market you're serving, you have a better idea what customers and prospects need from you. What will matter to them. And how you can serve them.

Next, we show how to keep marketing aligned with business strategy despite the incredible change in the audience.

CHAPTER 4

The Buying Team

Chapter Overview

For a lot of reasons, buying teams are growing by leaps and bounds in almost every industry. Major purchases, for instance, might involve a wide range of company functions, including Human Resources and Information Technology. But not all buyers are created equal. So it's essential to determine what role each specific individual plays on the buying team.

The Buying Team

Developing a clear understanding of the audience is one of the most important links between business strategy and marketing. If you know what your audience wants, you can see how those needs connect to your company and its products. You see how you fit in ... or don't. And you chart a course for getting your story out there. That's the essence of marketing.

But understanding the audience is equal parts art and science. And the ground is shifting constantly. Now, more than ever, marketers are faced with not a single buyer, but a buying team. And that team is growing, adding new members and points of view.

The growth in the size and complexity of the buying team is one reason why so many companies have turned to account-based marketing (ABM) approaches. Despite the name, marketing has been slow to catch up. More on this in later chapters.

The Growth of the Buying Team

One of the major changes observed over the past few decades has been the growth of the buying team. Where once there was a single buyer and maybe that person's boss, now there is a larger group of people involved. Not quite the Mormon Tabernacle Choir, but close.

There's good reason for that. The average initiative in today's organization impacts a broader segment of the business:

- It probably will touch enterprise-wide systems, for example. Thanks to the Internet of Things, a new machine for an assembly line has to be linked into a company's Information Technology (IT) system.
- A new machine may require special training to operate.
- It may require special care and handling, adding to the burden on the MRO team, the maintenance staff.
- It may help your customer's ongoing effort to comply with environmental regulations or safety protocols. Or hinder it.

The growth of the buying team means more people, more disciplines represented. And more information to communicate.

In *building products*, you can expect to have architects, owners, and contractors all in the mix.

In *building management*, owners, property managers, and tenants will all be represented.

In *health care*, you can expect to have team members from Human Relations (HR), nursing management, clinical services, and Environmental Health to physicians, patients, their families, and many others.

And, similarly, with *education*, you may be dealing with facility managers, faculty, staff, students, parents, alumni, taxpayers, and even the general public.

And those are just a few.

Your task is further complicated by the proliferation of communications media available to this larger group. While your company's marketing in the past may have focused solely on one or two trade journals, you now may have to consider a wide range of options (more of this topic in Chapter 7).

Plus, the ways to reach them have changed. Where there were once ads that were broadcast to the entire market, we now have media offering one-to-one interactivity and connectivity. As a result, audience preferences have changed too.

It all adds up to more people, more disciplines. Different learning styles and communications preferences. Less reliance on the relationships with sales reps. The same is true no matter what industry you're talking about.

Roles

It was the early days of the Customer Journey phenomenon. I was a member of a team that showed our client how an actual transaction might occur. We pointed out that there was an engineer with a need. They had supervisors to contend with. Peers. Then HR (for hiring and training), the maintenance-repair organization, plus environmental health and safety. Not to mention purchasing, finance, IT, and the shipping department.

By the time we had concluded, we had roped in almost everyone in the customer's immediate universe, except the washroom supervisor and the parking attendant. Maybe even them.

If our objective was to confuse our client, to paralyze them as they planned their next year's budget, we had succeeded admirably.

I felt as if there had to be a better way.

Not All Buyers Are Created Equal

With the addition of more players and more disciplines, the buying team has become even more of a challenge for marketing.

Some have advanced the idea that marketers should create separate marketing programs for each of the buyers on the team. And, in theory, they are right.

But that can get out of hand quickly, especially with an industry like health care, where you would need a minor league baseball stadium to get all of the team members together.

The good news is that, despite what it seems, the buying team is not an unruly mob. Not all of those buyers are created equal. Some have more influence than others, as is appropriate—as Gary L. Neilson, Karla

L. Martin, and Elizabeth Powers note,[1] the first key to strategic execution is clarifying decisions rights—identifying who owns and needs to participate in a business decision. Most buying teams (and companies) have worked those issues out, formally or informally.

As a result, these new buying teams are a lot more structured than they might seem. Different team members have different level of influence, depending on their job titles or responsibilities. Some have input only. They simply are included for awareness only. Some can offer advice or counsel, but are not involved in the final decision, which may rest with a small group or even one person. And some, hopefully a very small group, may have veto power.

Adapting the RAPID decision model advanced by Paul Rogers and Marcia Blenko,[2] we can group these people into four categories.

Influencers are people who are not directly involved in a project or initiative but need to know about it, as shown in Figure 4.1. Largely because they may be expected to accommodate some changes that happen as a result. Good examples might be HR people, who may not be directly affected by a decision to purchase a new piece of equipment but would need to help train or recruit skilled operators.

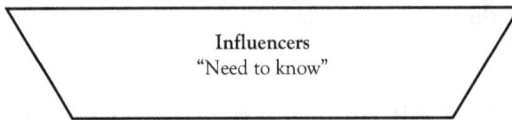

Figure 4.1 Influencers

[1] G.L. Neilson, K.L. Martin, and E. Powers. 2008. "The Secrets to Successful Strategy Execution," In *HBR's 10 Must Reads on Strategy (including featured article "What Is Strategy?" by Michael E. Porter)*, 100. Boston: Harvard Business Review Press. Kindle Edition.

[2] P. Rogers and M. Blenko. 2006. "Who Has the D? How Clear Decision Roles Enhance Organizational Performance," In *HBR's 10 Must Reads on Strategy (including featured article "What Is Strategy?" by Michael E. Porter)*, 151. Boston: Harvard Business Review Press. Kindle Edition.

Recommenders (see Figure 4.2) are coworkers who also are not directly involved in a proposed change but might have a stake in the outcome. The proposed change might be parallel to or directly affect their area of responsibility. For instance, packaging equipment might be affected by changes in the way a product is configured. Or that equipment itself might impact how products are sent for shipping.

Owners are the project champions, the people who have the most to gain or lose because the purchase directly affects their work. They usually organize the effort, creating the Request for Quotes (RFQs), compiling all the bids, and submitting the final proposal for approval. They are the main advocates for the purchase, but they may not have final approval (see Figure 4.3).

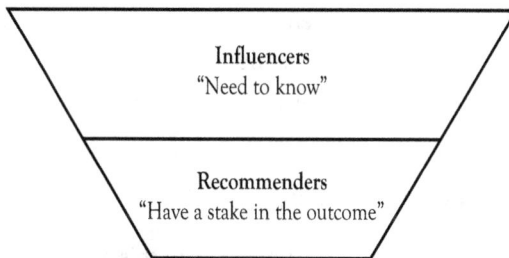

Figure 4.2 Recommenders

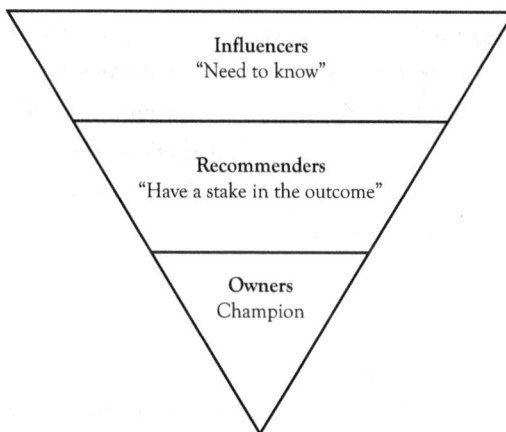

Figure 4.3 Owners

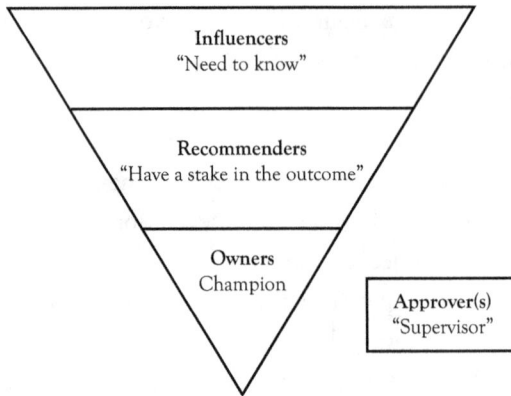

Figure 4.4 Approvers

Approvers are usually the supervisors of the project owner with direct responsibility for approving expenditures within a certain budget range. And while they may not be the final decision makers, they certainly have veto power, as indicated in Figure 4.4.

What That Means for Marketing

By classifying the members of the buying team this way, we can give marketing efforts an important boost. The key realization: Everyone does not need equal attention. Again following Neilson, Martin, and Powers,[3] the second key to effective strategy execution is information flow—making sure that the right information is available to the people who need it.

As a result, the next step is to determine what roles the various members of the team will be playing, as shown in Figure 4.5, and decide what information they will need to play their part effectively.

The entire team, as shown in Figure 4.6, needs some top-level information on the goals and the overall impact the project will have on the organization.

---

[3] G.L. Neilson, K.L. Martin, and E. Powers. 2008. "The Secrets to Successful Strategy Execution," In *HBR's 10 Must Reads on Strategy (including featured article "What Is Strategy?" by Michael E. Porter)*, 100. Boston: Harvard Business Review Press. Kindle Edition.

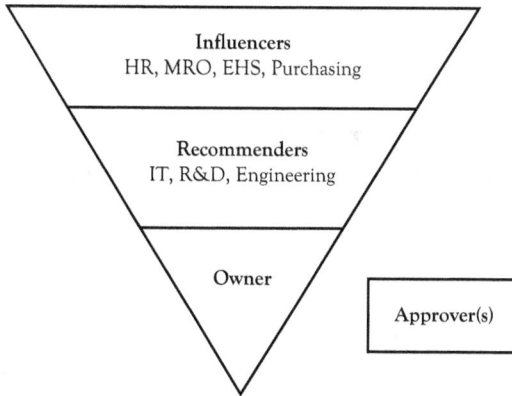

Figure 4.5 Depending on the kind of purchase, the roles on the buying team might look like this

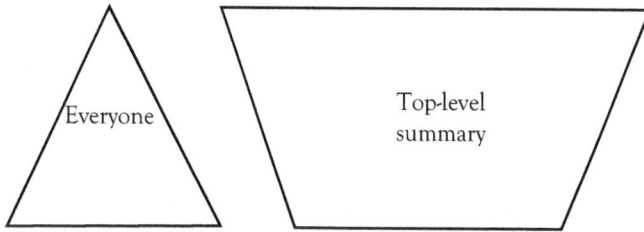

Figure 4.6 Top-level information goes to everyone

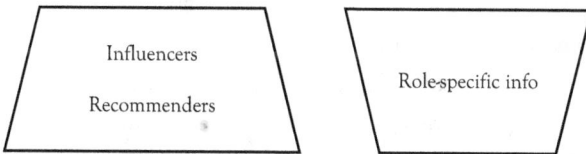

Figure 4.7 Influencers and recommenders need information specific to their roles

Next, influencers and recommenders will need to know some specifics for their disciplines. Like the IT protocols for the chief information officer (CIO). Or the training needs for the HR department. See Figure 4.7 for details.

Owners, of course, will need everything—a full proposal with costs itemized as shown in Figure 4.8. And, since they will most often be the focal point for the team, they'll need to have the packets of information

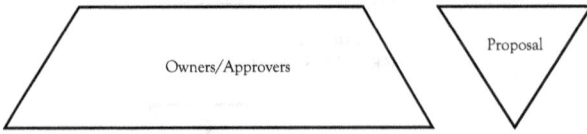

Figure 4.8 Owners and approvers, of course, need the full proposal

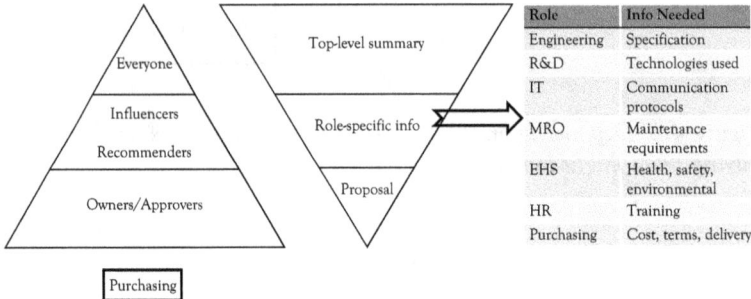

Figure 4.9 Examples of the kind of role-specific information that influencers and recommenders might need

disseminated to the influencers and recommenders. That way, they can respond to questions and resend information in the event the team members have lost or misplaced it.

Approvers, of course, will have final signoff. Their level of information will vary from one organization or even one situation to another. Some, most likely those who have placed their confidence in the owner, will simply need a quick summary. But a more hands-on manager may need to see everything that the owner sees, as shown in Figure 4.9.

Table 4.1 summarizes the information in chart form.

The one outlier is purchasing. In past years, purchasing simply handled the transactional details, perhaps beating a vendor up on price and nailing down delivery details. In many large corporations, however, the role of the purchasing function has grown much larger—forcing regular vendor reviews and requiring competitive quotes for any sizable purchase. And if the lowest-cost vendor is not selected, there had better be a good reason. And a high-level executive may have to take personal responsibility for the decision.

What Do They Need?

Table 4.1 Chart showing how the needs of a typical buying team may differ, according to their job responsibilities

Information needed	Approver	Decision maker	Rec: IT	I: HR	I: MRO	I: EHS	I: Financial
High-level overview	x	x	x	x	x	x	x
Engineering info	x	x					
Specifications		x					
Competitive advantages	x	x					
Maintenance		x			x		
Training		x		x			
IT communications protocols		x	x				
Safety features		x				x	
Environmental impact	x	x				x	
Cost/terms	x	x					x
Delivery	x	x					

Roles Change Constantly

The roles may vary from project to project, depending on the nature of the initiative. A good example would be the role of HR. If the initiative involves an update to an existing machine, for instance, the current operators may simply have to be retrained to take full advantage of the new features that are available. On the other hand, if the additional equipment required an operator with a higher level of programming skill, HR may need to play more of a recommender role, especially if those skills are not readily available.

Identifying the Key Player

The most important thing is to decide who the key player is. Who is going to pull the trigger? Who is going to decide what is best for the company and champion the cause up and down the organization?

On paper, it might look as if the project owner is the decision maker and that would make them the person to focus on. But sometimes the owner of the project is simply performing a clerical or coordination function and has little say in the final decision. That would make the approver the key person. In most cases, the decision is a shared one.

It often comes down, unfortunately, to who has the most to lose. Who will gain or lose clout, make or miss their bonus, gain greater authority or lose it?

It's critical to decide whom to focus on. When you decide, you'll want to create personas for the key players, to help keep your team focused on who you are talking to.

Personas

Playing tight end and wearing number 84 is …

Our client manufactured large pieces of construction equipment. And the distribution system was complicated, to say the least.

There were large rental companies who bought their equipment.

There were people who used their equipment on jobsites, usually renting it.

There were construction companies and industrial firms who bought the equipment for their own use.

And then there were institutional customers such as hospitals and universities, who bought their equipment as well.

And each of those different types of customers brought their own set of buyers and buying influences.

The rental companies had purchasing people. But they also had store managers at each of their locations. As well as sales reps who worked directly with customers to select the right equipment for the job.

On the jobsites there were foremen and equipment managers. Plus the workers on the site who actually used the equipment.

At hospitals and universities there were facility managers and maintenance organizations, as well as maintenance crews.

All in all, more players and more specialties than a college football team. And at various times, we had to connect with some or all of these players to help our client sell its products.

We developed personas for the top five buyers at first. And they became so helpful and useful; we were up to a dozen. Not only did we fill a PowerPoint slide with details and information, we actually made life-size cutouts that the client used to help them keep all the players straight.

They were even better than the program at that college football game.

Personas, Defined

Personas are fictional composites of the target audience, capturing some basic information about what a target audience wants, needs, and cares about (Figure 4.10). These descriptions enable your team to focus on the key characteristics of the audience, so they can better create communications that will connect. They are based on hard evidence: market research and depth interviews, leavened with some observations from your team in the field.

They humanize the audience, giving a face and a personality to your prospective customer. And helping your team develop understanding for your prospect, perhaps even creating a sense of empathy that sparks a better way to address the marketing challenge.

John Smith, Plant Manager

Age: 42
Communication preferences: E-mail, phone

John started at Amalgamated right out of college and worked his way up from process engineering, earning his MBA at night. He's assembled a crew of dedicated young engineers who have helped him improve the company's competitiveness and profitability.

Title
Plant Manager

Experience/Education
20 years in the industry
BS, MBA

Hot buttons
Improving product quality
Complying with regulations
Cutting costs

Influences
General Manager
VP of Engineering
R&D Manager

Information resources
Plant Manager website
Plant Engineering

Figure 4.10 A more detailed persona like this always needs to be available to the team

Creating a Persona

Traditionally, personas tend to be organized around the basic information about job title and role. But there's been a trend to develop profiles driven by psychographic or behavioral attributes. While the latter may be more revealing, they're hard to do if you're not intimately familiar with the audience, including the target market's roles, responsibilities, technologies, working environment, and clout within the organization. Most companies, especially B2B marketers, simply do not have research available to guide these decisions. And this is not the place to get creative.

As a result, I tend to favor a more basic approach. But there can be an evolution. You may be able to do a more elaborate persona when you acquire greater understanding (and research) about the people you are trying to reach.

A Basic Approach to Personas

First, start with the role. Go back to the organization we described in Chapter 3 and understand what is important for the place the target audience occupies in the market structure. This information will give you the framework for the most important part of the persona: the hot buttons.

Second, learn who they are. Find out what education and experience they will need to have to obtain their position. Are they teachers, nurses, engineers, or accountants?

Third, find out who influences them. Needless to say, their boss (and probably their boss' boss) play a major role in their lives. But what about their coworkers? Who reports to them? And are there parallel positions that might influence their selections of products or services?

Finally, you'll want to know where the audience goes for information and how your prospects stay in touch with their industry. The final version appears in Figure 4.11.

Working With Your Sales Team

It's important for marketing to coordinate with your sales organization. The presence of an agent in the field can help identify the players and determine how you need to communicate.

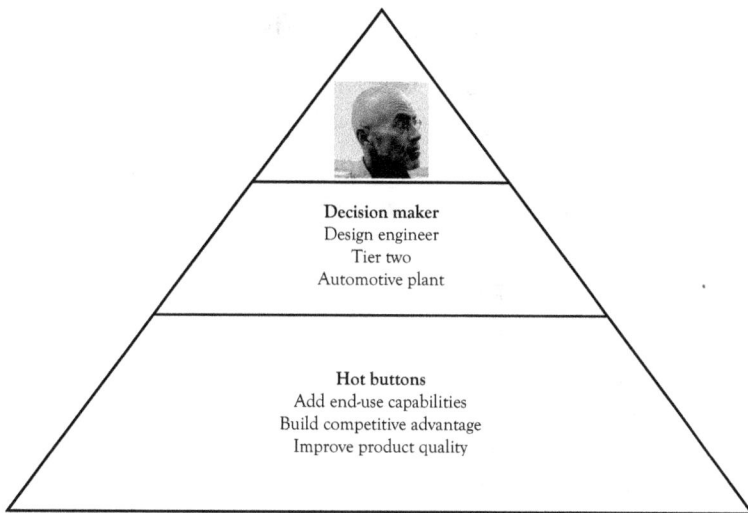

Figure 4.11 I like the use of short-form personas like this one to capture the key information. They're perfect for summaries or dashboards. And it will have many additional uses, as you'll see later

Sales reps can help you get a better feel for the psychographic information mentioned earlier, making your personas more real.

And, of course, mastering the structure of the buying team can help marketing managers support any account-based marketing (ABM) programs their organization has undertaken. Doing successful ABM, where marketing and sales work together to identify and communicate with specific prospects, requires close coordination with sales. Both ABM and the marketing and sales relationship are worthy topics but go beyond the purposes of this work.

Chapter Summary

Points to Remember

- The buying team is growing by leaps and bounds.
- Not all buyers are created equal.
- The role a person plays on the buying team determines what they need.

Advancing Brand Vision

Understanding the audience is critical to the process because it directly connects your business strategy to your marketing. It draws a straight line connecting your company, its goals, and its aspirations to your customers and what they need and want. The stronger the tie between these two, the greater the chance of success.

It's important to emphasize that you cannot fudge the truth here. While it might lead to some short-term benefit, being less than honest will have long-term consequences—showing that you can't be trusted. That would be fatal.

Next, we show how to communicate with your audience, developing a storyline and messaging that will resonate.

PART III

Creative: Concepts That Captivate

Development of marketing creative is one of the most important steps in the process of connecting business strategy to marketing tactics. It is, in fact, where the wheels often come off, as everyone from the creative team to the executive board falls in love with a concept that is cool. Or hip. Or whatever. But misses the point of the strategy.

That's the problem of falling in love with a story that doesn't go where you need it to go. And that usually happens when the creative starts before the strategy is defined. As if you can rationalize the creative into the strategy. Or, worse yet, retrofit the strategy around the concept.

That's the point of developing a strategic vision first. The clear-eyed, declarative sentence that not only says what you need to say for the task at hand but also flows naturally out of the business strategy and positioning.

Many would say that's not possible. That the only way to get good creative is to let your imaginations run freely. That's baloney.

Great creative begins with great strategy. Period. No matter how fun or cool the creative, if it's not on strategy, it's useless. It may even be harmful.

CHAPTER 5

The Story

Chapter Overview

The story is an integral part of your marketing efforts, the tip of the spear, telling the world who you are. But the problem isn't that most companies don't have one. The problem is that they have more than one. Marketing has its story. Sales has another story. Individual reps may even have their accounts. So a company should create a strategic vision capturing what it needs to communicate. With a story that is aligned, connected, and differentiating.

Getting Your Story Straight

Several years ago, a new client came to me with a familiar tale. They had tons of datasheets, they said. They had a website. They had some great customer testimonials. And they had multiple divisions, all working very diligently to provide outstanding products and services for customers.

"We have all that information," the client said. "But, we need a story." I knew what she meant. She was partly right. But in some ways, she wasn't.

Even if you haven't been marketing, you have a story—at least one. There's the C-level business strategy story. There's the story your customers tell their colleagues. Your marketing story. The stories your sales reps tell. And, Lord knows, your competitors have been telling stories about you since you first entered the market.

For the most part, you have stories, all right. You have them out the proverbial wazoo. The challenge is to reconcile them. Get them all as close together as possible. And infuse them with reality. Make them authentic.

Your CEO might think he can dictate your story. And he can, sort of. He can tell your people what he wants them to say. Have it printed on every piece of marketing literature. Make employees recite it every day when they come to work. Put it on your website.

But will that work, and will it be true? Will every sales rep tell the story to every customer? Will every customer believe it, and will they tell their friends? Probably not. And not even the most confident CEO can make it so.

For most companies, the problem is like that of our client. They have the stories, tons of them. They just don't know the right one to tell. They probably don't know what their sales reps are telling their customers or what those customers, in turn, are hearing. And because none of your people know what they are supposed to say, your marketing literature, product sell sheets, and website probably all tell different stories.

As a result, you may not know your story, but you have one. You have at least one. And if you ever hope to have a clear line of sight between business strategy and marketing tactics, you have to get your story straight.

Your story is the tip of the spear. It tells customers who you are as a company. Explicitly or implicitly, it promises benefits. It talks about real advantages they can use to improve their products or services to their customers. It gives your employees a rallying cry, a mantra that all your people should have in mind as they go about their daily tasks. From the shop floor to the sales counter to accounting to research and development. It offers a sense of pride and purpose, maybe even giving your employees a reason to come to work in the morning. It helps recruit the next generation.

In marketing, your story provides focus, and a sense of direction to all your communications, both internally and externally. It drives integration, giving all your messages a familiar look and feel. And it motivates your creative team, whether it's an internal team or an external one.

For all these reasons, you need a story—one story. And you need to get it right.

That's where the creative process comes in. Giving you the story, the images, and the words that, for a positioning piece, captures who you are and explains that to your audience. Or for a product promotion, it explains how a product will benefit the customer, and why you're so perfectly suited to bring it to market.

The Strategic Vision

One of the routine questions in market research is to ask what's important to the audience. Especially, how important each of the main values is to them.

As a result, when I was doing the project mentioned in Chapter 2, I dutifully asked my interview subjects to tell me how important it was that their chemicals supplier was innovative. I expected the traditional, "it's great," and "Oh that's really important." And we got a few of those.

But when I probed deeply, I found a surprising number of customers weren't all that crazy about innovation. Yes, they needed to make cost improvements and, yes, they needed to improve performance, by changing their processes.

But they weren't all that crazy about trying new chemicals or totally new processes. Far from it.

"Try out the new stuff on someone else," one customer told me. "I don't want to be your guinea pig."

And he was not alone. A sizable number of customers just weren't buying into the idea.

The good news was that several of the company's competitors were all in on innovation. Using the positioning pyramid we introduced in Chapter 1, we found that they were all clustered at the top of the pyramid, around product and technology leadership, as shown in Figure 5.1.

Their bigger and more entrenched competitors were thus jockeying for the same place in the competitive landscape. A place that customers didn't find all that alluring.

I went back through my mountain of interview transcripts and even conducted a few more. Fortunately, I had asked every subject some general questions about what they valued about our client.

The responses were all different. The client's techs, my interviewees said, helped them lower costs. Boost production. Address environmental issues. Cut waste. The list went on and on. Even those who were positive about innovation defined the term not as developing new products and technologies, but as being creative in finding solutions to a variety of application problems.

Product/Technology
leadership

Competitor A

Competitor B   Competitor C

Competitor D

Operational   Customer
excellence   affinity

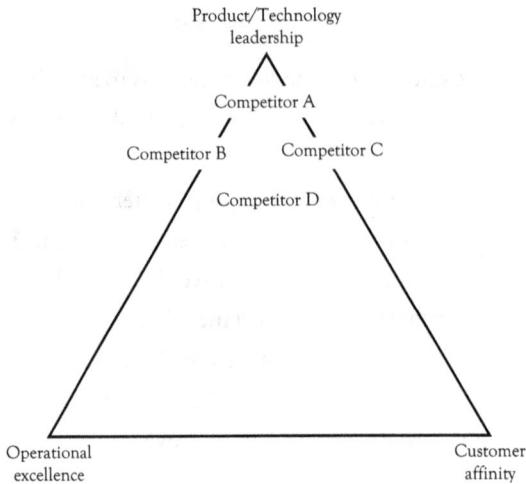

Figure 5.1 *All of my client's competitors were clustered around the Product and Technology leadership position*

For a while, I was worried. There were a lot of loose threads. But then, a pattern emerged. The interview subjects emphasized what I started calling *outcomes*. Time after time, interview after interview, the same phrase kept coming up:

"They help me solve problems."

I went back over the interviews and discovered that more than half of the respondents had said that phrase, in one form or another. And the company's strategic vision was born.

Strategic Vision

The strategic vision is the linchpin of the *Brand Vision* process. It is the keystone connecting the business strategy and objectives, the audience need, and the marketing creative. It is not quite the same as the business strategy or the business objectives, though it needs to reflect those points.

It is rather a succinct statement capturing what the marketing program needs to communicate. When you're finished, it's the thought that lingers, the substance you want the audience to take with them. To retain.

And though we've talked mostly thus far about branding-level communications, these principles apply to product- and market-level campaigns as well. The major difference is that branding directly references and reinforces the positioning, while the strategic vision for a market or product program is a step removed, illustrating how an initiative supports the brand position.

How Do You Develop the Strategic Vision?

While I've always felt that defining the Strategic Vision for a project was relatively straightforward, it always seems to get a little complicated in practice. But there are a few steps that I think will make it a lot easier.

This isn't an exact science, for sure. But these steps should get you where you need to go.

Start With the Category

What kind of product or service are we talking about? And at what level? Is this a project defining the brand or launching a new product? Since branding is a little more straightforward, we'll use a product as an example. Specifically, a control system for a machine, The Bumpkins 3000.

What Are the Primary Advantages?

Usually, the answer from the client will be a laundry list of advantages:

- It's cheaper.
- It's faster.
- It's smaller.
- It's more efficient.
- It's more accurate.

Many marketers stop there. Proclaiming "The new Bumpkins 3000 is smaller, faster, and cheaper." Or something similar. Then everyone will debate about whether the order is correct and whether the other two advantages should be included as well.

That won't cut it, because we really don't address the customer's concerns.

Convert the Advantages to Benefits

With your client's help, you'll want to convert those advantages to benefits. Why does it matter that the Bumpkins 3000 is faster? In this case, the increased speed gives the machine designer a greater level of control. Because it is more accurate, it allows greater precision. And because it's more efficient, it saves energy.

Once again, a rush to judgment would give us, "The new Bumpkins 3000 gives you greater control and more precision, also saving energy."

Better, because we're talking customer benefits. But still a hodge-podge.

Connect With the Audience

In their discussion of customer value propositions (CVPs), James C. Anderson, James A. Narus, and Wouter van Rossum[1] point out that many marketers simply list all the benefits of a product, including some that aren't important to the customer. To do a CVP correctly, they say, you should camp on the benefits that matter most to your target audience.

At this point, then, it's smart to look at our persona, developed in Chapter 5. What matters most to them?

First, the power use of the control system is a relatively small fraction of the energy consumption of the machine. So that's not something that they really will care about that much.

Second, the control and precision would be important to a machine designer. Depending on the type of machine they're making, the improved control could enhance operator safety. Meanwhile, the greater control precision could allow them to build a machine that achieves tighter tolerances or makes more elaborate motions.

Looking at the persona, we see that safety is not specifically mentioned, though we know that it is important. But the ability to build a machine that does more—and does it with a higher level of precision—could well

---

[1] J.C. Anderson, J. A. Narus, and W. V. Rossum. 2006. "Customer Value Propositions in Business Markets," *HBR's 10 Must Reads on Strategic Marketing (with featured article "Marketing Myopia," by Theodore Levitt)*, 113 Boston: Harvard Business Review Press. Kindle Edition.

allow them to build competitive advantage into their machine. And we know that is a big deal from our persona.

You will at least be able to say "The new Bumpkins 3000 allows you to build competitive advantage." And, that matches well with your position as a technology leader, so it's a great fit with your corporate strategy as well.

That connects our audience hot buttons and the corporate strategy. So now we're getting somewhere. But maybe we can go even further.

Finally, Make It As Differentiating As Possible

Understanding the competitive environment, what is the strongest statement you can make about the new Bumpkins 3000?

What we had earlier isn't bad. At least there is something the audience will respond to.

But can you say more? You'll want to take a look at the persona again to see if there are any clues there.

And can competitive products achieve the same level of accuracy and speed? If not, you can make the statement even stronger:

"No control system is better at helping you build competitive advantage."

Much better.

Remember, that that's the strategic vision. It's not intended to be a headline. Admittedly, it could be. But the intent is not to create headline copy. It is to create absolute clarity. Like Gadesh and Gilbert's 80–100 rule, mentioned in the introduction to the strategy section.[2]

In fact, in the situation described in the opening, one of our client contacts objected to the use of the word "problems" in the strategic vision. They felt it was too negative and suggested "challenges."

But I presented two points: First, I was using the customer's language. The company, they said, was solving their problems, not their challenges. They raised the issue, not me. Second, I didn't say it, but it sounded too much like the HR department talking. And third, I pointed out that the

---

[2] O. Gadiesh and J.L. Gilbert. 2001. "Transforming Corner-Office Strategy into Frontline Action," *HBR's 10 Must Reads on Strategy (including featured article "What Is Strategy?" by Michael E. Porter)*, 128 Boston: Harvard Business Review Press. Kindle Edition.

strategic vision was not copy. It would certainly not be used in a headline and probably not even in the body of an ad or web page. It was intended as straight talk, pure and simple. Marketing, not HR.

It stayed.

Strategic Vision: A Summary

In short, your strategic vision needs to have three key characteristics as shown in Figure 5.2.

It needs to be **aligned** with the business strategy and objectives. It should be clear how the strategic vision will achieve at least one of the business objectives. And, of course, it needs to clearly show how the project embodies the business strategy. In the case of the Bumpkins 3000, the introduction of an advanced technology demonstrates you're a product leadership company.

It needs to be **connected** to the audience need. Specifically, it needs to address at least one of the audience hot buttons. As noted earlier, the Bumpkins 3000 helps a design engineer reach a new level of sustainable competitive advantage.

And finally, it needs to be **differentiating**. That means no one else has the new technology and can make the same definitive statement about the benefits the product conveys. Because no competitor has a product offering the control and precision of the Bumpkins 3000, we can definitely say that it allows a design engineer for an original equipment company

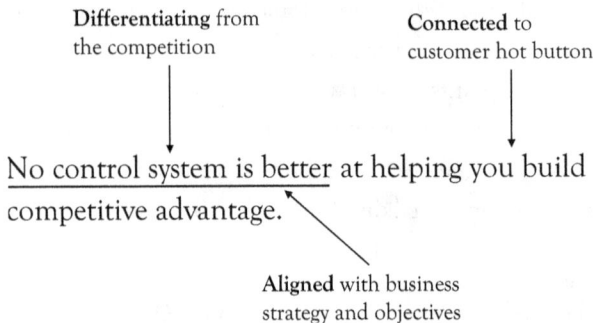

Differentiating from the competition

Connected to customer hot button

No control system is better at helping you build competitive advantage.

Aligned with business strategy and objectives

Figure 5.2 The strategic vision needs to be aligned with the business and connected to a consumer hot button. Finally, it needs to help you differentiate your company from competitors

(OEM) to build in competitive advantage. And no one else has that new technology and it is patented.

Rosser Reeves coined the term Unique Selling Proposition (USP) in the 1940s to move competitive advantage to the forefront in marketing communications. A strategic vision structured in this way is a USP on steroids. It has the USP's differentiation, but the alignment with the business strategy and objectives and the connection to the audience hot buttons makes it a strategic powerhouse.

Note that the statement is blissfully short. It has no weasel-words, no touchy-feely, feel-good corporate malarkey. It's not a headline, just a clear and concise statement, with a single compelling idea.

What Makes a Good Strategic Vision?

Your goal for the strategic vision is to develop a short phrase summarizing the key benefits your company provides to the market.

But don't try to reach finished copy during the session. If something catchy comes up, great! Write it down. But you don't want your team of pyramid builders to get bogged down in group copywriting. Let that to your creative team.

Remember, however, that your strategic vision is not a slogan or ad line, not a design or graphic standard. It's not copy or artwork. It is, in fact, the driving force behind all of those things.

You want to make sure the strategic vision is clear and definitive and avoids corporate-speak. All too often, someone tries to throw everything into the strategic vision. Every possible buzzword, every concern or issue the company thinks it needs to address. And the strategic vision ends up being wishy-washy or unclear. Nothing dooms a market or branding effort faster than that.

"Sustainability," for instance, is a concern often raised during these sessions. But while that may be a hot-button issue, it is rarely a deciding factor for a customer, primarily because it is not differentiating. Most competitors in an industry are at parity, so it's rare that one company has a competitive edge or at least one that's sustainable. It might be a good thing to have, for sure. But it is not usually a deal-breaker or motivating factor.

Chapter Summary

Points to Remember

- Your story is the tip of the spear, telling the world who you are.
- The strategic vision captures what you need to communicate.
- It should be aligned, connected, and differentiating.

Advancing Brand Vision

By nailing the strategic vision statement, we make a clear and compelling connection between business strategy, audience hot buttons, and the market needs, as represented by the differentiation.

Next, armed with the strategic vision, you'll next want to sketch out the content.

CHAPTER 6

The Content

Chapter Overview

Content is a major part of the business marketing process. By providing the information a prospect or customer needs, it offers evidence proving the claims a company makes in its marketing materials. This chapter introduces a process to gather that information and present it in the most compelling way possible. And it presents a Creative Brief summarizing strategy, audience, and messaging.

The Content

Content has always been important in marketing. Especially solid, thought leadership content that provides valuable information a customer can use. The kind of information that gets picked up quickly on Google and is read and reread thousands of times.

It offers evidence of your claims about your products or your company. Solid information that a technical person or expert can review and evaluate to determine the accuracy of your claims and whether (or not) you have the expertise you claim to have. You can think of it almost as a third-party endorsement.

But content creation isn't easy. And many marketers have difficulty with content development, especially with technical topics.

That's why *Brand Vision* makes content development a central part of its approach. And it finds ways to create content more efficiently. The process is called pyramid messaging.

Pyramid Messaging

Based on logical, rational, deductive reasoning, pyramid messaging gives your marketing materials the structure and the information that informs them and makes them strategically relevant.

It involves the creation of a single document that captures all the information relevant to a project. It creates a source document, providing the building blocks of content you need to construct your marketing program, from web pages, PR articles, and brochures to videos, e-mails, and social media posts. It's done once but is used and reused countless times, as long as a subject has marketing relevance.

Pyramid messaging is a key tool in achieving integration and consistency across the entire program, even if the elements are created by different people or even different organizations.

The goal is to create a single source that can be used by anyone developing content for the program. All the information is captured and approved at once, making the process much more efficient for your subject matter experts (SMEs).

All marketing tactics then can be developed using approved content. That should at least simplify technical review, if not eliminate it entirely. The goal is to put in the effort up front to collect, clarify, and confirm the information, so that the back end of the process—the marketing implementation—can happen more efficiently.

Having a source of approved content also enables quick responses to topics that seem to crop up on a regular basis. Giving you, for instance, the content to respond to a press inquiry, fodder to comment on a blog post, or grist for the insatiable appetite of social media.

Pyramid messaging also gives marketers a resource to respond to the content needs of marketing automation or ABM systems. And it supports the need for content for training, customer service, or other uses.

Advantages of Pyramid Messaging

Invaluable. A single source used by anyone.

Efficient. Created and approved once, to make the best use of your SME's time.

Agile. Enables quick responses to industry topics.

Versatile. Used for anything from training and customer service to marketing automation and ABM.

Building SME Star Power

SME access is a serious issue, especially for technical topics. For good reason. Your SMEs are the top minds in your company. Your franchise players. And their time is valuable. When they're not in a lab developing a new technology or working with manufacturing to implement a new product development project, they're flying around the world to be with customers, solving real-world problems. You don't want to waste their time.

And while it is true that the SME is doing you a favor by cooperating with your inquiry, you are helping them as well.

First, you're taking several important steps to make sure you're making the best use of their time. You're capturing all the information at once and working with them to make sure it's accurate. So they don't have to be bothered afterward as the campaign of paid ads, Tweets, e-mails, and videos rolls out.

Second, by organizing a campaign around their specialty (and them), you're elevating their status in your organization. And third, if you're both successful, you'll make them a media star in the industry. And SMEs love media attention as much as anyone else.

You can think of pyramid messaging as a poor man's knowledge management system, capturing valuable information that's currently available only from your SMEs. And it makes the best use of all your resources, both your budget and staff time.

The core document in the process is the messaging pyramid.

Messaging Pyramid

The main objective of the messaging pyramid is to summarize the strategic vision for the project and present the evidence that supports the claim. This will be the core idea that your marketing team will want to present to your audience. And have your target persona remember.

It starts with the strategic vision. We'll use the introduction of the Bumpkins 3000 control system as our example (see Figure 6.1).

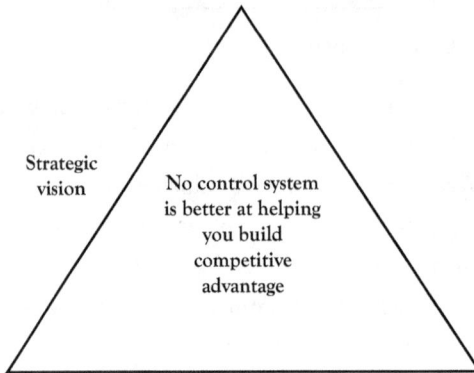

Figure 6.1 The messaging pyramid starts with the strategic vision

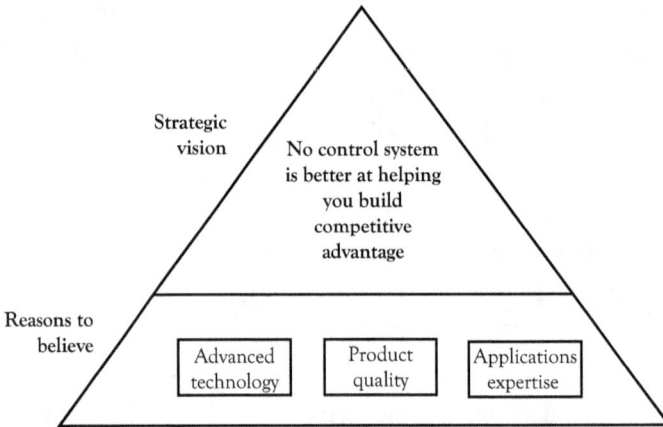

Figure 6.2 Next, add in the reasons to believe

Then we develop three to five reasons to believe that unequivocally prove the strategic vision (see Figure 6.2).

Some companies require that the reasons to believe for an individual project be the same as for the overall corporate messaging. That's a bad idea in my view.

As long as the project itself supports the corporate strategy and business objectives, the messaging you develop will help the company the most by forcefully presenting the case for the project. That's much better than trying to force-fit the project's reasons to believe under the corporate umbrella.

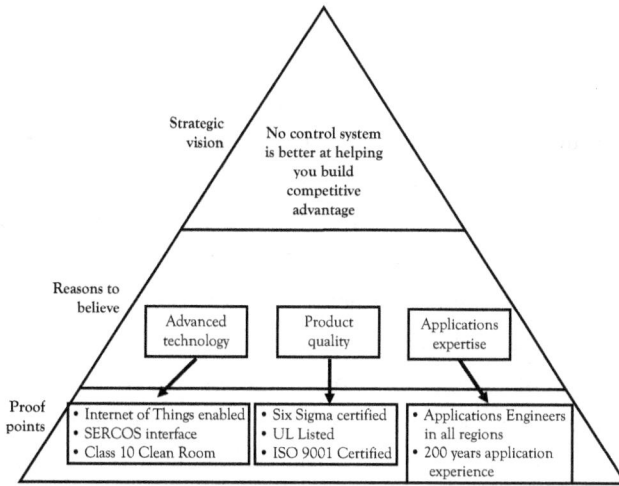

Figure 6.3 The proof points support the reasons to believe

Make no mistake about it, a messaging strategy exists for one reason only: to close the deal, to make an unassailable case for the strategic vision.

At the next level, you'll want to add proof points to present the evidence confirming the reasons to believe (see Figure 6.3).

It's a good idea to send this document to the client for approval. After you have signed off on the messaging pyramid, you'll want to tackle the master messaging.

Master Messaging

The master messaging is where the process gets serious, creating a single pyramid messaging document that captures all the information needed to complete the project and states it in a consistent way. It should be reviewed and approved by all the key decision makers, especially the SMEs. It then provides approved content that copywriters and content creators will use to develop the creative materials that will become the promotional campaign.

It's organized in much the same way as the pyramid messaging document, stating quite clearly the strategic vision, the reasons to believe, and the proof points. But it provides much more detail. Because of the additional information, master messaging is created and delivered in a word processing document.

It should provide specific points like case histories or other types of detail confirming the reasons to believe. As well as a definition of terms, especially for more technical topics. Plus it is a good place to include a few "short subjects," 100-character starting points for social media posts.

Master messaging should not be viewed as finished copy, but close. Rather, it is the source content that all of the media creators will use. It ensures that they are starting with the correct information and the preferred phrasing for the descriptions of products or services. It is therefore more objective and straightforward—not as promotional as the final copy will be.

Final copy, of course, cannot be created until the creative concept is developed, which is the next step in the process. But having the definitive description of the product or service that is contained in the master messaging is a huge help to the creative process.

It should be written clearly and concisely, addressing all the issues, defining all technical terms and jargon, and explaining the benefits of the product or service in detail. It should provide the level of detail needed

---

Who Should Write the Master Messaging?

Harried and torn in multiple directions, marketing managers often find it difficult to give a project's content the attention it needs. Especially in the area of technical content. Most likely, they'll want to have someone other than an engineer or SME work with them to develop these critical documents. That means, for the most part, that it should be prepared by a professional writer, not an engineer (unless they are a distant relative of Billy Shakespeare). After all, the reason these documents need to be created is that the technical folks are too close to the subject. It's not the best use of their time and they're not writers.

Only a skilled writer can span the distance from the technical detail to the high-level overview of what the product is and how it fits into the customer environment. That's the best way to ensure the content is clear and definitive. And covers all the ground you'll need for your project. The writer should understand your strategy thoroughly and be familiar with the various media you want to consider. And they should be comfortable working with technical topics and experts.

for any element of the promotional program, including white papers or technical articles.

Integration

By giving the content creators approved explanations that clearly define the advantages of the product or service, pyramid messaging gives marketers a lot of flexibility in harnessing the skills of a wide range of media specialists in creating the final materials they use.

And it gives those content creators the freedom to customize the presentation of the content to meet the specific needs of their medium, whether it's a Facebook post, e-mail, space ad, or white paper.

The result is a more integrated program. One that will perform better because all the members of the choir are singing from the same song sheet.

Creative

Few areas of the marketing process are more fraught with difficulty than the development of creative communications. If we are to believe some, that's understandable: the rationality of the business mindset coming up against the free-form thinking of an artistic mind.

And yet, the marketing communications we are discussing are designed to further commerce, not art. That doesn't mean that marketing materials need to be dull or boring. Decades of experience prove the opposite.

But the creative pieces must meet the business needs of the project, or else there's no reason for it to exist.

The purpose of this book is not to tell companies or marketing firms how to become more creative or how to structure their creative organization. There are many other works that cover that material. Rather, our purpose is to make sure marketing materials deliver on the business strategy and objectives and connect with the audience.

We'll start with the creative brief.

The Creative Brief

The creative brief is perhaps the most important document in the creation of the program or campaign. It provides the direction for the team of writers, art directors, and content creators who will develop the campaign.

Not surprisingly, it needs to summarize all the information we've captured and show how the project connects with the process we've described thus far.

Let's walk through the process of building a creative brief. Rather than use a branding-level program, as we've done earlier, we'll show how the process works by stepping through a product-level promotion. The main difference? Rather than asking "What does the brand stand for?" but rather, "How does this product or market initiative support the corporate positioning and embody the brand?"

Who Are You?

You start with the summary of the business strategy. In this case, we'll use the introduction of the Bumpkins 3000 control system as our example.

The team will need to know the positioning established by your business strategy efforts (see Chapter 1). The positioning goes at the top of the pyramid, as shown in Figure 6.4.

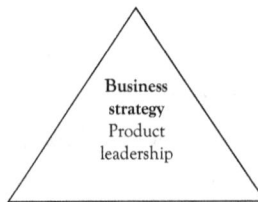

Business
strategy
Product
leadership

Figure 6.4 Business strategy

Then you add in the business objectives (Figure 6.5).

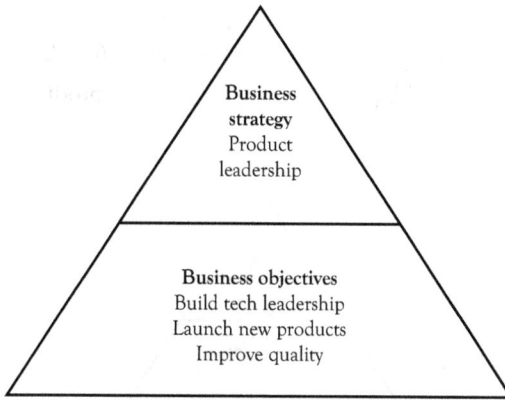

Figure 6.5 Business objectives

Next, you summarize the audience concerns.

Who Are You Talking To?

You'll start with the audience discussed in Chapters 3 and 4. And you'll want to decide how many personas you need to concern yourself with. Probably, you won't go after the entire buying team, unless you have Apple-sized resources. You'll probably need to pare it down (no pun intended). So rather than a purchasing person, whose job is to find the best price and terms, you might target a key influencer: the user of a machine, for instance. Or a safety manager, for a product that reduces fall risk.

You'll want to capture the key elements of the audience and the persona you've created for the key decision maker, which in our example is the design engineer, shown in Figure 6.6.

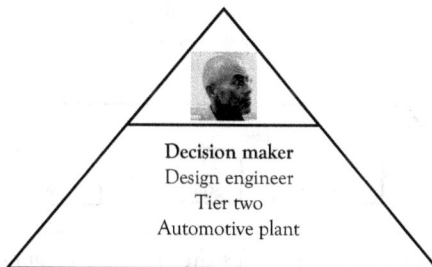

Figure 6.6 Identify the decision maker

Most importantly, you'll want to highlight the audience hot buttons at the bottom of the pyramid as shown in Figure 6.7. In this case, our design engineer is looking for ways to improve his product and make it more competitive.

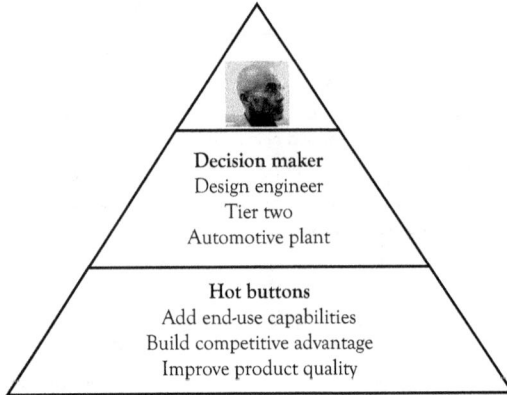

Figure 6.7 Add in the decision maker's hot buttons

What Do You Want to Say?

You'll want to include the messaging, which summarizes the strategic vision and the reasons to believe. The messaging (as shown in Figure 6.8) clearly shows the Bumpkins 3000 has the ability to give design engineers some important tools they can use to improve their products.

Figure 6.8 The messaging includes the strategic vision and reasons to believe

The Full Brief

Putting it all together, you'll have a creative brief with all the information your creative folks need to get started. It summarizes the business situation on the left, the audience setting on the right, and then captures the messaging in the center of the brief, as shown in Figure 6.9.

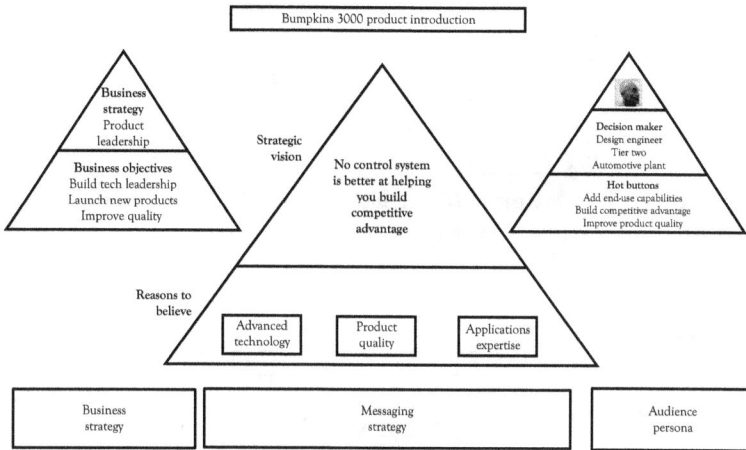

Figure 6.9 The full creative brief

The Connections

It's easy to see how the pieces of the puzzle connect and interrelate. As shown in Figure 6.10, on the business strategy side of the brief, the Bumpkins 3000's advanced technology supports both product leadership business strategy and the business objective of building technology leadership.

And, of course, the project supports the corporate objective of launching new products, as shown in Figure 6.11.

On the audience side of the brief, the fact that product quality is a reason to believe supports the key decision maker's goal of improving the quality of his own products (as shown in Figure 6.12).

In addition, the advanced technology could well help our decision maker add end-use capabilities and build competitive advantage (as shown in Figure 6.13).

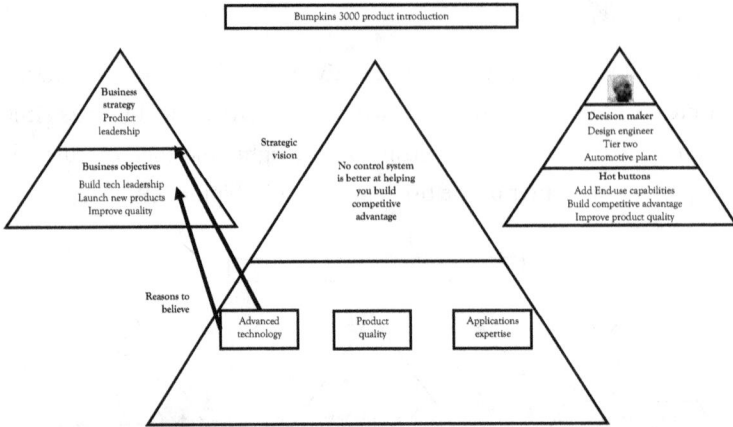

Figure 6.10 *The advanced technology point in the messaging supports both the business strategy and business objectives*

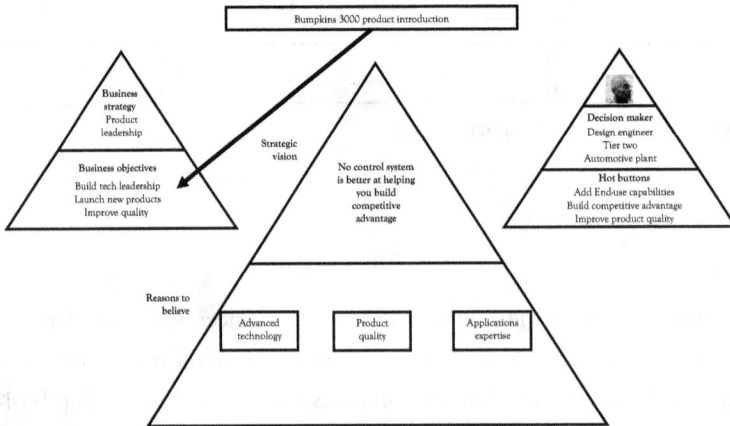

Figure 6.11 *We see the project itself supports the business objective of launching a new product*

The same is true of the applications expertise, the company's ability to customize the way the product is applied in a specific application (as shown in Figure 6.14).

The strength of the brief is in its ability to summarize the communications objectives and show at a glance how the project supports the business strategy and objectives. And how it connects with audience concerns.

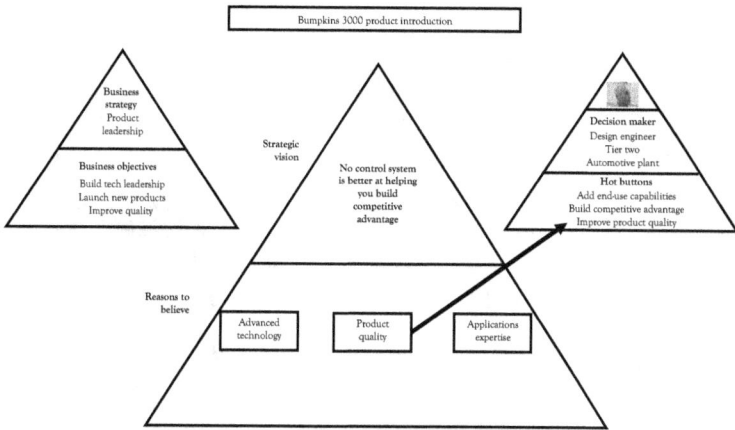

Figure 6.12 *We see that the Bumpkins 3000's high level of quality will appeal to the design engineer's desire to improve product quality*

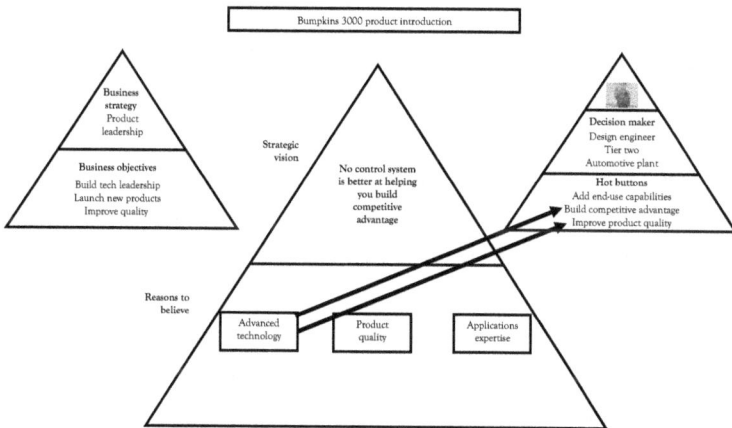

Figure 6.13 *Once again, the advanced technology of the Bumpkins 3000 should help our decision maker build competitive advantage*

Armed with a creative brief, you're ready to begin the creative process. Once again, the purpose of this work is not to suggest ways to enhance an organization's creativity, but rather it is to make sure the creative team has the tools and the direction to produce work that meets your company's needs.

Appendix A contains a template to develop a *Brand Vision* Creative Brief.

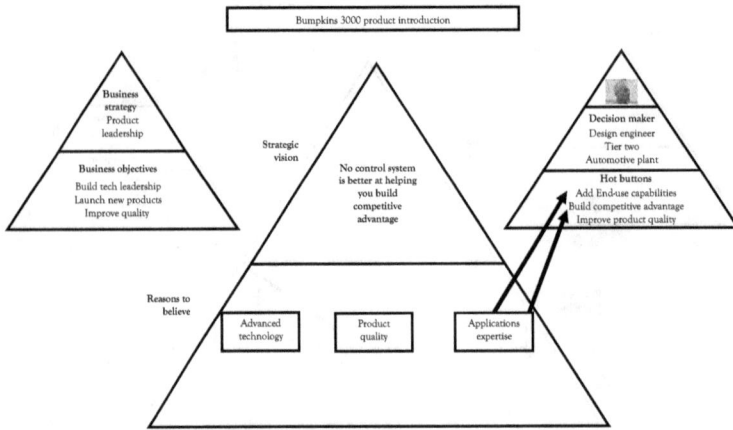

Figure 6.14 *The ability to customize how the Bumpkins 3000 is applied should also add end-use capabilities and help build competitive advantage for the customer's product*

The Creative Process

The process is fairly straightforward.

It begins, of course, with the brief, mentioned previously.

Next, it's always good to have an input meeting where the strategist reviews the brief and makes sure the team understands it. In my experience, this step is absolutely critical.

All too often, marketers create briefs that leave some points open to interpretation. The writer of the brief, for instance, might have picked up too much technical jargon and copy-and-pasted it over to the brief unexplained and unfiltered. More likely, they didn't perceive an issue raised by the creative team. Or they tried to finesse it.

No matter what the cause, these issues must be resolved, either by the strategist or, ultimately by the client and the SME.

It must be crystal clear. No ambiguities. Period.

Why is that so important?

I've seen far too many creative teams churn indecisively, wasting countless hours dealing with ambiguities of one sort or another. And the results of the process reflect that. Far better to go back to the client to resolve the issue.

There were a few cases where the marketer admitted that they didn't know the answer to the question raised by the creative team. In one case, a new technology, neither the marketing manager nor the product manager knew the product's selling advantage, debating between elevating a specific feature or promoting the product's ability to be field customized.

Rather than give the creative team an ambiguous charge, I chose to divide the team and have one half working on creative addressing the product feature while the other half focused on the customizability. Both concepts went to the client and the presentation of opposing creative approaches helped the client resolve the issue.

After the creative team has the opportunity to brainstorm, it presents its concepts to the creative director. And, after the concepts are refined to their satisfaction, the creative directors then present to the client, with the support of the team.

One important addition: Have a mantra. Chan and Mauborgne point out in *Blue Ocean Strategy*, it's important to have a simple, straightforward phrase that absolutely nails the selling advantages of a business strategy. The same is true of creative approaches.

The more memorable the phrase is, the more likely it is to gain traction and make an impression on all your audiences, both external and internal. Plus, the right phrase can be repeated almost anywhere, from an ad and a Facebook post to a web page and an e-mail. Think "Only pay for what you need" or "Fifteen minutes saves you ..."

Making the Process Work

There are a few basic principles that help ensure the success of the process. The main rule is that everybody needs to play their position. And the team needs to have enough time to do good work.

In marketing, there's an unfortunate tendency on the client side to see the creative process as their personal sandbox. A place to play. Change this color. I don't like that person's smile. Is the type big enough?

Whether they're an agency account exec or strategist or a client marketing director, the person who makes the decisions on the design and wording of a marketing communication is the creative director, no matter what their title or company affiliation. And, in my experience, people who play outside their area of expertise are playing with fire. Asking for trouble. And weakening the final outcome. Design decisions belong with design professionals, it's just that simple.

A marketer wouldn't dream of asking an engineer a question about the size or the performance of a product. Or ask a company financial officer if their calculations are correct. So why do they do that with a creative product?

Here's a simple thought: If you're not comfortable or happy with the creative product you're getting, get someone else. Everyone will be better off in the long run.

To make the process work the best, reviewers should focus on a few key points:

1. Is It True to the Strategy?

    Does the creative nail the strategy? Does it reinforce the positioning? For instance, if your company is a product leadership company, does the communication exude performance? Does it bristle with technical competence?

    And does it address the business objectives? If, for instance, you're trying to establish your company's thought leadership, does the concept tell the audience something they may not know?

    Finally, does it fit the brand? Is it in character? Is it something your company could or would say?

2. Will the Audience Relate to It?

    Given what you know about the audience, will your target prospects respond to this communication? Will it hit them where they live? Will it offer them something they simply can't ignore?

    If the creative meets these two objectives, reviewers should not inject their personal preferences. It's all about trusting the team to come up with the best creative solution. And, of course, giving the team time to do its work.

Chapter Summary

Points to Remember

- Content has always been important in marketing and is central to the process.
- It offers evidence proving the claims you make in your marketing.
- The *Brand Vision* Creative Brief summarizes strategy, audience, and messaging.

Advancing Brand Vision

Having a clear, concise brief helps the creative team achieve a laser focus on the business strategy, business objectives, audience needs, and messaging. It's a document the team should focus on from the beginning to the end of the project. And having a rational process follows right behind, maximizing everyone's contribution to what is a complex effort.

Next, we talk about the incredible variety of media choices that offer opportunities to market your products.

PART IV

Campaigns: Marketing That Orchestrates

No Silver Bullets

Marketing managers are assailed continuously by one sales rep or another touting the benefits of the latest tool or technique—Twitter or Instagram? Marketing automation or programmatic advertising? Paid search or e-newsletter ad?

Who is right?

The answer is, of course, they are all right—sort of. The different tools do work, do help produce sales in many cases.

But they are all wrong in one crucial aspect: None of these tools work alone. They need to be connected.

They all require other tactics, other media, to seal the deal. People who are touting one approach or another don't want to talk about that, because that doesn't help them close the sale. But that doesn't make it any less true. In fact, it's always been true.

Even in the *Mad Men* days in the 1960s, it never was true that consumers saw an ad on TV and miraculously bought the product. They always had to go to a store or at least call a toll-free number to complete the sale. Other forms of marketing still were involved—in-store merchandising, at least. And probably even store promotion (so the retailer could let you know they had the product).

And it's even more true now. Customers may purchase a product online. But, most likely, they start with search. They then go to a website to execute the purchase. But, before that, they also routinely look at reviews. They might check in with their friends or peers on social media. Watch a YouTube video of the product in action.

The point is that none of these tools are silver bullets, despite what their advocates say. They all need to be connected.

CHAPTER 7

Media and Integration

Chapter Overview

Today's marketers use a wide range of media to get their messages out to their audiences. But, for some, this cornucopia of choices is a curse rather than a blessing. The key, once again, is remembering that all of these media tactics are tools, not strategies. And their greatest strength is that they can be connected. That allows marketers to organize all these media choices into campaigns that advance the sale.

Media

In 1964, Marshall McLuhan famously proclaimed that the medium was the message. He recognized that books and magazines are fundamentally different from broadcast TV or radio. And live theater was something else yet again.

Electronic media represent yet another significant milestone in human evolution. They add new dimensions to our ability to communicate. They put a wealth of information at our fingertips, making it available 24 hours a day. And they are interactive, adding a whole new realm of capabilities.

These new choices offer additional tools and even outcomes, allowing users to select among video, games, text, animations, even virtual or augmented reality.

And that presents a wonderful opportunity—an invitation to review the options and select the best vehicle for the message. Marketers now have a variety of different tools to tell our stories. We can be more selective, more sophisticated about our use of these media than were the communicators in the past.

Shiny Objects

With all these new choices thrown at them, however, it's easy for marketing managers to get distracted by the latest shiny object. To become fixated on one medium or tool to the exclusion of others.

Admittedly, the choices can be mind-boggling: Social media such as Twitter, Facebook, and Instagram. E-mail, snail-mail, and print advertising. Display ads, video, organic and paid search. And, of course, the Internet itself, with nearly six billion indexed pages and counting.

In his book, *The Context Marketing Revolution,* Mathew Sweezey uses the term *infinite media* to describe the situation we face.[1]

Media Proliferation

Perhaps in response to this proliferation of choices, the media landscape has become subdivided. With such a wide range to cover, it may have been inevitable. But it's too much. It's caused the field to become siloed, splintered into different spheres of influence. With many companies having a separate e-mail strategy. A web strategy. A social media strategy. And even a Facebook and a Twitter strategy.

What is wrong with these companies' various media strategies is that they have them in the first place. All these media are tools, admittedly great ones. But tools don't have strategies.

Most likely, the separation of the media into different turfs is a way to meet production demands. Or it's done for budgeting purposes.

But separating the media into these separate fiefdoms destroys one of their most valuable assets—their connectivity.

Connected Media

We are in a new era of connected media—communications hyperlinked to deliver a unique, customized experience to every user. An experience the user drives.

---

[1] S.S. Mathew. 2020. *The Context Marketing Revolution: How to Motivate Buyers in the Age of Infinite Media.* Boston, MA: Harvard Business Press Books.

That means a social media post has a link to a product announcement. An e-mail links to a landing page. A testimonial quote links to a full case history. Sparking interest, giving the audience a chance—and a reason—to find out more.

If you're not thinking about the pieces an individual communication connects to, you're missing a huge opportunity. You're wasting money. You're probably disappointing your audience. You're undermining your marketing efforts, and you're possibly losing the sale.

To take full advantage of the connectivity of the interactive media, marketers need to select from the incredible buffet of choices and fashion a mix of different tools to tell their stories. Achieve their objectives. And sell products.

How do you do that? The key is knowing how to capitalize on the unique strengths of the individual media.

Assessing Media Strengths

The media that marketers have available to them—even the new ones—are not all created equal. They have their strengths and weaknesses that marketers need to factor in and use to their advantage.

Various media experts have done exhaustive analyses of the overall strengths of the different media, so there's no need to repeat that. For our purposes, however, it will be most beneficial to look at these platforms through the lens of marketing. And determine what marketers need and use terms appropriate to the task at hand.

The Connect–Convince–Convert Model

The attractiveness of the latest shiny object is certainly one of the major hurdles we encounter in marketing communications today.

I've seen a client who committed a major investment to an e-mail-only campaign. I've even seen a client choose to do most or all of his marketing on Twitter.

Those one-note campaigns rarely work.

Why? Because one medium can rarely do everything you need it to do in a marketing effort. E-mail might reach your existing customers. Twitter might get the story out quickly.

But you need more than that. You need a comprehensive plan to reach prospects and customers who may be interested. A forum to provide them information that shows them your company has something to offer. And a way to turn them into a customer.

That's where the Connect–Convince–Convert model comes in.

The CCC Model

We'll start by looking at the main tasks you need to accomplish and see how the various media options at your disposal can help us.

First, you need a method to disseminate new information. To get the word out about your new products or services. We call this phase of the process, "Connect."

Second, you need a place where interested prospects can come to find out more. We call this phase, "Convince."

And third, we need a way to reach out to customers who have expressed interest. We call this phase, "Convert."

Let's talk about each phase in a little more depth, giving some examples of appropriate media choices at each level. Note that these are examples only. Not only are new media channels and types emerging constantly, but the capabilities of existing media are evolving as well.

Connect Phase

The goal of the connect phase is to deliver your message to your audience, whether you are introducing the company itself or promoting a new product or service. You'll want media choices that quickly reach as much of your target audience as possible. Advertising leaps to mind, whether you're talking print, online display ads, or paid search. For the same reasons, public relations is helpful, adding a third-party endorsement when placed in a leading publication or website.

You could also use direct marketing (e-mail or snail-mail). You might alert your existing customers, for instance, when you are launching a new product. But, if you are introducing the company itself, either because of a new market initiative or a merger, you will probably have to purchase a list of names to reach people who are not known to you but are nonetheless in your prospect category (generally less useful than using your own list).

There's also programmatic advertising, the automated sales platform that identifies specific targets and serves up advertising as individual prospects surf the Internet in both their business and personal pursuits.

Paid media tend to have an advantage in situations like product launches, where you need to get the word out quickly. Inbound marketing advocates will point out that that's not cost-efficient. And, of course, it isn't. But it's a question of being pennywise and pound-foolish. A few weeks can make a critical difference in the profit earned through a new product initiative, both in cementing and capitalizing on competitive advantage. And in recouping the company's investment, before competitors have the opportunity to respond. New product development, after all, can cost in the tens of millions of dollars, if not hundreds. The money spent to get the word out rapidly is chump change by comparison.

Convince Phase

During the convince phase, your goal is to provide more information, fulfilling the prospect's desire to find out more after seeing your ad or banner in the "connect" phase. The Internet, of course, is the most logical place. But it could also be a catalog or brochure. Or you could interact live, at a tradeshow or on a sales visit.

The more technical the product, the more relevant the raw data becomes. Engineers, for instance, love datasheets providing all the product specifications. Or white papers, explaining any new technology. In less technical settings, product application videos or stories may be helpful.

And in any setting, customer case histories and testimonials are very helpful, especially if you can name a high-profile customer who used your product or service. Getting the prospect to watch videos or hear testimonials from satisfied customers is pure marketing gold.

Convert Phase

When a prospect is in the convert phase, you'll want to reach out to them and offer additional resources—some juicy new pieces of content—to help them make their decisions. Since "convert" messages usually need to address specific needs or applications, direct communications like e-mail or even a sales call are a natural.

Generally, this has been the realm of a company's sales function (reps, dealers, or retailers). But retailers have had to reduce their knowledgeable sales staff. Industrial companies have pared back the number of reps. And this qualification and nurturing function has more and more passed to marketing. To make sure a lead is "ready to buy" before it is passed along for sales follow-up (and investment of company time and resources).

Marketing automation tools can also provide prospects with timely responses and more detailed information. They can follow up when a person has stopped progressing toward the end goal of buying or asking for sales help. Your objective, of course, is to be viewed as helpful, not intrusive. Informative, not salesy. It needs to feel like help, not harassment.

You could also offer premium content, like a calculator, proprietary research study, or e-book. Most likely, you would put that information behind a firewall and require a user to break anonymity—providing contact information.

A Word on Social Media

Because of the unique nature of the platforms, social media are in a special category. Or, more accurately, they can be in all three phases.

You could and should send out new product announcements on Twitter. Many companies use their Facebook pages as more of an inquiry fulfillment device than their web pages, and messaging features on all the popular platforms allow the same level of personal interaction as direct marketing.

For most companies, however, the primary function of social media will be a little more basic. They'll want to build and maintain a relationship with a loyal following, a role that lightly crosses over the three stages. In most cases, however, you'll need to take a prospect to the Web (or even a sales call) to complete a transaction.

As a result, too many companies' use of social media is fraught with problems. To keep their posts "fun," their social media pages are full of high-level messaging, mostly unrelated to markets or products, but producing very few leads or sales.

These companies wonder what is wrong with their Facebook or Twitter "strategies." The problem is that they're attracted by the "free," 24-hour accessibility and easy-to-use interfaces, allowing the demands (and limitations) of the platforms to shape the message. And thus, Facebook, Twitter, or Instagram *become* their marketing program.

We've probably had enough experience by now to verify that that doesn't work. The solution is that social media posts need to be connected, part of an ongoing marketing program planned and optimized to deliver results.

We'll talk about that next.

Putting It All Together

A marketing initiative needs all three phases, connected and working together to generate leads and sales. All the levels have to be in place to cover the prospects' information needs, deliberately moving a potential buyer from one step to the next.

Apportioning costs among the three levels is a complex effort tailored to the brand's unique strengths, the marketplace, and the offer. It is an inexact science, customized for individual markets, companies, and even products, putting it well beyond the scope of this effort. The most important thing to note is that the allocation process needs to be optimized by the results the program delivers, a point discussed in greater detail in Chapters 9 and 10.

The inverted pyramid shown in Figure 7.1 captures the three phases, with the pyramid on the right listing the media most effective at reaching individual prospects. They are also summarized in tabular form in Table 7.1.

Admittedly, it is shaped like a funnel, driving a prospect through the sales process. And we use our insights about the customer journey to help us to create exciting content that virtually *compels* prospects to ignore the distractions occurring around them and move to the next phase of information discovery.

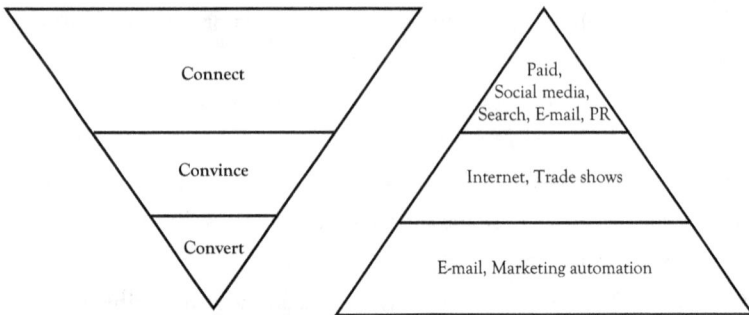

Figure 7.1 While the pyramid on the left looks like a funnel, it's first and foremost an information discovery device. And the pyramid on the right provides examples of media that achieve the goals of the three stages listed on the left

The Three Phases: A Summary

Table 7.1 A summary of the three phases that a marketing initiative needs to be successful

Phase	Function	Media Examples
Connect	Introduce your company to the audience, convey your positioning, and promote new products or services, reaching as many eyeballs as possible.	Ads, PR, social, e-mail, search, social media
Convince	Give the audience the opportunity to obtain more information about your company, your product, or your service.	Website, trade show, sales visit, social media, brochure, catalog
Convert	Initiate direct contact with the prospect, following up, if possible, on their specific interests or pain points.	Marketing automation, e-mail, sales call, social, direct marketing, social media

Integration

A client came to me with an unusual challenge. There was a one-year backlog on the company's flagship device, known for its high quality and world-class engineering. Meanwhile, it had significant capacity in another area, in a product line that was almost a commodity.

How could the company alert the market to the new capacity without compromising its reputation as a supplier of quality and world-class engineering? The plan was to market the product at a price point and delivery that was aggressive by any standards. But especially so in light of the premium pricing and one-year wait for the flagship product. On top of that, our client had a limited budget and an urgent need to generate sales.

I had been working on a concept that I called the "lean lead machine," designed for precisely this kind of situation. It put the three-phase, Connect–Convince–Convert model on steroids, promoting the commodity's availability while preserving the corporate positioning. The client loved the idea, and we began developing it.

The "machine" we created organized a full range of "connect" media under a headline reading, "Brand X Quality in 5 days." It included paid search, organic search, online ads, and e-mails into an integrated package of tools that quickly blanketed the market (what Stephen A. Greyser, and Robert F. Young called integrated marketing communications[2]). The campaign drove prospects to a landing page where they could fill out a form.

The project was a big success, with orders surpassing the cost of the program quickly. It succeeded for two reasons. First, we made sure all the media were connected, as mentioned previously. And second, we thought of the effort as a campaign.

No Longer Just Tactics

The critical distinction in this program was that we were no longer focusing on isolated tactics but were thinking of a coordinated campaign designed to produce leads. And we worked with it until it achieved that goal.

We even took the "machine" analogy to the point where we scaled the media buy up and down, based on order flow. When a lot of requests came in, we slowed down the ad placements, turning the campaign on again when orders started slowing down.

---

[2] S.A. Greyserand and R.F. Young. 1994. "Cunard Line Ltd.: Managing Integrated Marketing Communications," *Harvard Business School.* https://hbsp. harvard.edu/product/594046-PDF-ENG

The program was so successful that the client added more budget to keep it going. And we later did a very similar project for a related product.

The key to our success was the campaign thinking, the mindset that viewed the project not as a series of isolated tactics, but as a "machine" that we had built to generate leads. With marketing viewed as just another production input, shown as revenue in and revenue out. It was something our manufacturing-oriented clients could understand.

Campaigns: A Definition

As a result of the experience mentioned previously, I recognized that campaigns are a way of organizing all the media choices we now have at our disposal. And creating a comprehensive, integrated instrument to connect, convince, and convert.

Admittedly, business marketing campaigns don't usually have the glamour of business-to-consumer (B2C) campaigns. There simply aren't multimillion budgets for Super Bowl commercials or prime-time television. But there is an important similarity—both use thematic repetition and frequency to drive home marketing messages. So, once again, no mass media budgets. But tons of repetition to a smaller audience—think Adwords, banner ads, e-mail, and social. Even public relations.

A few other key characteristics of a program:

- A common objective, like a new product launch, new market initiative, acquisition, promotion/sale, even a brand refresh.
- A consistent look and feel, with shared visuals, graphics, and type. A common voice and tone. And shared values.
- A measurement component designed in, not added as an afterthought. So that we can know immediately if the campaign is working. And have some idea what needs to happen, if it isn't.

Most importantly, though, the individual tactics need to be organized into a package that consciously moves a prospect through the process, advancing the sale.

Who Drives the Process?

The most important person in this scenario is the decision maker. It's a person who is not mired in the details but is totally engaged in the big picture (and responsible for it). That means they are focused on three key areas:

1. **Alignment with strategy.** Does the creative stay true to the strategy? All too often, decision makers get lured into the sandbox, assuming the role of design critic. That's not the role here. Assume you have skilled designers and writers who have considered all the options and presented the best for review. And if you don't, you'll need to find someone else to work with.

2. **Integrating all media.** Are the Facebook posts, e-mails, articles, and ad insertions consistent with the campaign and true to the objectives? Not just that they look the same, feel the same, and deliver the same message. But that they work together to achieve the campaign goals. That requires a person who is conversant in and comfortable with all the media. Even showing a command of them all.

3. **Overseeing the results.** If you're the decision maker, you're responsible for the outcome, good or bad, so you need to ask yourself the hard questions. Is the campaign working the way it should? And are there ways to make it work better (see more in Chapter 9).

There really isn't exactly this role right now. But it could be filled by creative directors who manage to lift themselves beyond the creative considerations. Or it could be an agency account manager or client-side marketing manager who rises above the tactical world where they now play. Or it could be a new role entirely.

Breaking Down the Silos

The key is that it's not one media tactic or another. It's a mix of elements, capitalizing on each platform's unique strengths to tell your story. Try not to be attached either to the old or the new. Because:

- Nothing is faster than Twitter;
- Nothing is more universal than Facebook;
- Nothing is more convincing than a testimonial or case history;
- Nothing builds credibility like the placement of an article in a respected website or publication;
- Nothing gives you more control than a paid placement;
- Nothing catches the prospect when they're beginning their research as well as search (paid or organic);
- Nothing is more personal than an e-mail.

Why Campaigns Are Important

Campaigns are a recognition of the reality that there are no silver bullets. Despite what their proponents say, no social media platform, lead-gen device, or video-enriched landing page can do it all. Tactics, in other words, do not produce sales and leads, despite what their boosters say.

Only campaigns do that, by tightly integrating a package of tactics into a comprehensive program built and optimized around a specific objective. To achieve a specific goal.

Without campaign thinking, marketers can lose sight of the end goal. They can lose focus on achieving their business objective.

In addition, marketers have known almost from the beginning that consistency and repetition pay big dividends. Prospects rarely respond the first time they see a message, so organizing marketing efforts into campaigns increases the likelihood of success. Because no matter where or how they see it, they're getting the same message.

Chapter Summary

Points to Remember

- Media are tools, not strategies.
- The unique strength of media now is that they are connected.
- Marketers need to organize media into campaigns that advance the sale.

Advancing Brand Vision

By coordinating the efforts of all the various media and aligning the marketing direction with the corporate strategy elements such as positioning, audience, and messaging, campaigns advance *Brand Vision* and the goal of making sure marketing reflects the corporate strategy. As we shall see in Chapter 9, they build accountability into the marketing program as well.

Next, we learn how to build a campaign, following seven steps.

CHAPTER 8

Developing Campaigns

Chapter Overview

Planning a marketing campaign is a lot like being an orchestra conductor. You have to harness a wide range of personalities and skills, getting the best possible performance out of each player. And getting them all to work together to harmonize their efforts, with the whole being greater than the sum of its parts. This chapter offers a seven-step guidebook for the marketing orchestra conductor, going from planning through optimization and reporting.

The Orchestra Conductor

Dealing with a wide range of personalities, some heavy and serious, others flighty and capricious. Following a careful script but adding nuances and subtleties. Balancing the drive to create both artistic and financial success, with reputations and large investments riding on the outcome.

In all those ways, planning a marketing campaign is almost like being an orchestra conductor. It requires careful planning. Selecting the right instruments. Building a team. Coordinating an eclectic group of people. And executing flawlessly.

Campaign planners have to pick the right medium for the message. They have to help craft and optimize both the creative and the media mix. They have to work with media specialists as well as creatives to develop tactics that are optimized for the media, have on-target messaging, and advance the sale.

They have to focus relentlessly on moving the prospect to the next logical step, optimizing the tactics and the entire campaign to achieve the business objective. And, most of all, they have to apply what they've learned to the next campaign.

The process is relatively straightforward with seven key steps described as follows.

Campaign Planning in Seven Steps

1. Plan
2. Meet
3. Map
4. Create
5. Produce and launch
6. Optimize
7. Report

Plan

Because of the wide variety of media involved, campaign development requires both people with creative skills as well as many different specialists in paid placement, social media, public relations, e-mail, and so on.

Since there are so many moving parts, the tendency right now is to silo all these efforts, leaving them to develop independently. That's a disaster for business strategies, branding, and return on investment (ROI). And leads to marketing with zero effectiveness. Or at least a fraction of what it would have.

Campaign planning starts with the creation of a core planning document.

The Core Planning Document

Begin by outlining the initial steps in the strategy, especially your company's positioning, message, and audience. It starts with all of the key issues outlined in the Creative Brief, which was described in Chapter 6. The key questions are shown in Figure 8.1.

Who Are You?

The team will need to know the positioning established by your business strategy efforts (see Chapter 1). And it will help them to know who the competitors are and what positions they occupy (see Chapter 2). And, if

The question	
1. Who are you?	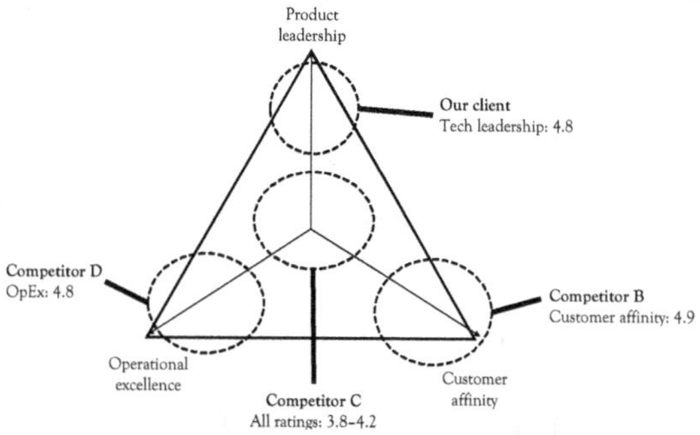
2. Who are you talking to?	**John Smith, Plant Manager**  **Title** Plant Manager **Experience/education** 20 years in the industry BS, MBA **Hot buttons** Improving product quality Complying with regulations Cutting costs **Age:** 42 **Communication preferences:** E-mail, phone *John started at Amalgamated right out of college and worked his way up from process engineering, earning his MBA at night. He's assembled a crew of dedicated young engineers who have helped him improve the company's competitiveness and profitability.* **Influences** General Manager VP of Engineering R&D Manager **Information resources** *Plant Manager* website *Plant Engineering*
3. What are you saying?	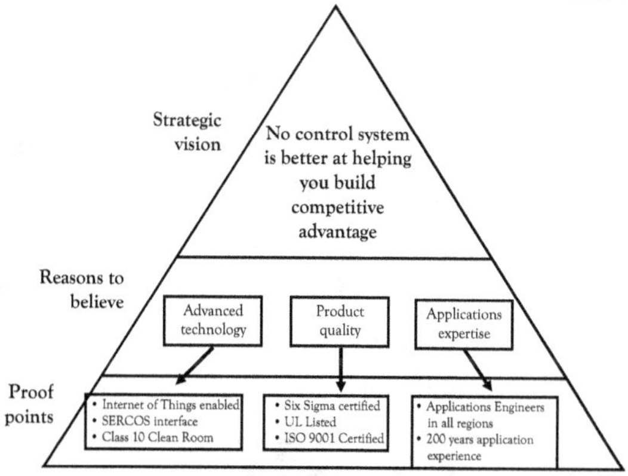
4. What do you want to happen?	Leads/sales 100

Figure 8.1 Campaign planning starts with the creation of a core planning document

the project is at the product or market level, the team will need to know what your rivals are saying about that particular topic.

Who Are You Talking To?

You'll list the audience (described in Chapters 3 and 4) and you'll want to focus on an individual persona, which you will share with the team. Your media experts will need to know about the prospect's media consumption and learning preferences.

And while you're focusing on a few key players, you probably want to list any special information that other buying team members will need from marketing. A good example is making the IT people aware of the data protocols a control product supports. Or any special regulations your product complies with; for example, UL (formerly known as Underwriters Laboratories), the Occupational Safety and Health Administration (OSHA), the Food and Drug Administration (FDA), or the Environmental Protection Agency (EPA).

What Do You Want to Say?

Include the messaging document, with the strategic vision, the reasons to believe, and the proof points.

What Do You Want to Happen?

You'll also want to identify your end goal or intended outcome, whether it's a sales qualified lead (SQL), a sale, a tradeshow visit, or a request for a sales call. It's important to be as specific as possible: 200 leads, $10 million in sales, 200 trade show visits. Admittedly, if you haven't established goals this concrete before, it will be basically a wild-ass guess the first few times. But you will be able to get more accurate with experience. And the practice will become extremely useful in the future, as you plan for and budget campaigns.

How do you do that? Much, of course, depends on the industry and the size of the audience. But knowing the goals can help you frame expectations and establish appropriate outcomes and budgets.

An important part of the process is estimating an expected rate of return. As with the end goals, you will not have a good idea of what your targets should be for your first projects. You'll need to have some experience actually running several campaigns and getting results. But you can start with industry benchmarks as a guide, understanding that you'll really need to replace them with your own experience as soon as possible.

Typical results throughout the industry, for example, might be a 10- to 15-percent click-through rate for e-mail to a cold list. Conversely, it might be only 0.25 to 0.50 for ads (maybe a little more for well-targeted programmatic ads).

And while those may be industry benchmarks, I always recommend that you develop your own. The reason is that response rates will vary by industry, by medium, and even by product offering within your company. The goal, of course, will be to develop the level of performance you'd expect for each and make more accurate estimates for the next round of campaigns.

The ability to do those estimates, coming up with reasonable guesses about response rates and ROI, could well be one of the most valuable assets marketing can create, other than the brand; more on that in Chapter 10.

Budget and Schedule

It's best, of course, if budget and schedule can evolve over the course of the project. But the reality is that they often come first, before any project planning or development can take place. In these cases, it's a matter of coping with and trying to live within the budget and schedule parameters that have been established.

Unfortunately, the typical response is to cut corners in the process, eliminating important up-front preparation like a kickoff meeting and the involvement of a full staff. That always is pennywise and pound-foolish.

The best approach is to go through the initial steps as outlined, making sure the team is aware of any challenges. Any number of things can happen: The team can come up with an extremely effective approach that saves money. They can come up with such a compelling program the client digs deep to find the money. Or the program can be broadened to encompass an allied product, approach, or initiative that can make the expenditure of additional time or resources worthwhile.

When you've completed the core planning document and established budget and schedule, you're ready to assemble your orchestra.

Selecting the Team

First you'll need a creative team including a creative director, a writer, an art director, a front-end designer, and a lead developer.

You'll also need a team of specialists to come up with the right media to use for your campaign. The most practical choice at the moment is to include experts from the obvious alternatives such as paid media, search, e-mail, social media, and analytics for at least the first round of your effort.

Ultimately, there will be a pitch-off where the specialists representing all of the media choices present their ideas about how the campaign might role out in their particular specialty. Then you select the best, most complementary alternatives for the final campaign.

Meet

When the campaign planning document is complete and your team is in place, you'll want to have a kickoff meeting to get everyone started and on the same page. Many consider this an unnecessary step, or at least an optional one. But failing to get the team together is always more costly, causing a lack of coordination and virtually eliminating the possibility that the program will be integrated. And assuring it will be ineffective.

At least in the initial stage, you'll have a crowd the size of a Rolling Stones concert, so you'll want to keep it brief. No more than a half hour.

You should provide the planning document to the team at least 24 hours before the meeting and ask the team to come with suggestions. And bring bribes—donuts or candy—any kind of treats or surprises.

Start the meeting by having the strategist review the planning documents and answer any questions. Ask them to keep it to 10 minutes, max, and focus on a few key points that give the team insight into the task at hand. Allow the group to ask follow-up questions and make sure everyone knows where to find all the background information.

Then, you'll want to give the team a chance to have a brief discussion about possible tactics or directions. Take the opportunity to do some blue-sky thinking, some spit-balling to get people thinking. If possible, initiate a dialog. You'll want the creative types to discover what the media specialists have to offer and vice versa. Your goal is to send the team off with a good attitude and a collaborative mindset.

Schedule the next meeting, allowing enough time to get together and complete the work. And get them ready for that session by explaining that they should come prepared to map out the campaign.

Encouraging Collaboration Across Channels

Media experts and creative types are not accustomed to working with each other. They have always been separate, perhaps working on different floors, in different buildings, or different companies. Possibly even on different continents. Might as well be different planets.

But to take full advantage of the possibilities the communications revolution has made available to marketing, it's more important than ever to break down the silos and create working relationships among the team members.

For example, knowing the creative team is planning to recommend a video illustrating how a product works would be a benefit to the media planners. They could well find many outlets for that video. And understanding the different social media possibilities available for that particular application might help creatives.

(For more on managing talent in creative industries, see Anita Elberse's article, "The Creative Industries: Managing and Marketing Talent, Module Note."[1])

---

[1] A. Elberse. 2011. "The Creative Industries: Managing and Marketing Talent, Module Note," *Harvard Business School.* https://hbsp.harvard.edu/product/509078-PDF-ENG

Brainstorm/Generate/Illuminate

Inspired by your meeting, your team is ready to get started. You'll want to send them off to work on their separate tracks. Hoping, of course, that they will communicate with each other and continue the collaboration you sparked at the meeting. And find ways to turn separate tactics into a powerful marketing campaign.

The Creative Track

Your creative team has a number of challenges to address. Their attention, of course, will immediately be drawn to the concept.

Their challenge will be to develop a concept that enlivens and illustrates the strategic vision your company selected, in Chapter 5. How can they dramatize it and make it come alive?

Beyond the core concept, however, there are some new, campaign-driven tasks for them to complete. For example, how are they going to tell this particular story across all the media? How will they orchestrate various tactics to convince the prospect to take the next step and find out more? How are they going to use the various media options available to them to roll out the message? Bring it to life? Live it?

One key consideration they will need to share with their media counterparts relates to the structure of the campaign. Will it have an anchor piece of content—a video, e-book, white paper, or research study—that proves your company's expertise? That will prompt prospects to take a major step—going to a store, agreeing to talk to a sales rep, or providing their identification?

And they'll need to think through the sequence of steps they'll want your prospect to take to advance the sale.

Will there be a teaser for a big announcement like a merger or a new, high-tech product? Will you provide bits of information leading up to a big unveiling at a press conference or trade show? Or will there be flights or waves of creative, sequentially building your case?

The more the creative team can describe the process they envision and share it with the media specialists, the stronger the campaign will be. Their goal, following strategy guru Michael Porter (from Chapter 1), is to make the program like the product, totally unique to your company. So distinctive, in fact, that it is almost impossible for the competition to imitate.

The Media Track

Meanwhile, your media people should be reviewing the media opportunities for each stage of the process like those shown in Figure 8.2. And they should look for placements unique to the specific application. Are there any new choices or media channels that the audience might be using?

For the **connect** media, what is the mix of ads, PR, social, e-mail, search? Are there other, better choices? Other media channels they can find, from an industry-sponsored community to a LinkedIn discussion group?

What's the best place to put the communications that will **convince** prospects? Naturally, a website is an obvious choice. But there are also trade shows and even sales visits.

Finally, to **convert** the prospect who has expressed interest but hasn't taken action, they'll probably be thinking of e-mail, marketing automation, social, or a sales call.

Social media isn't the answer to everything. Yes, it's free. But there are issues, such as proprietary concerns and even credibility.

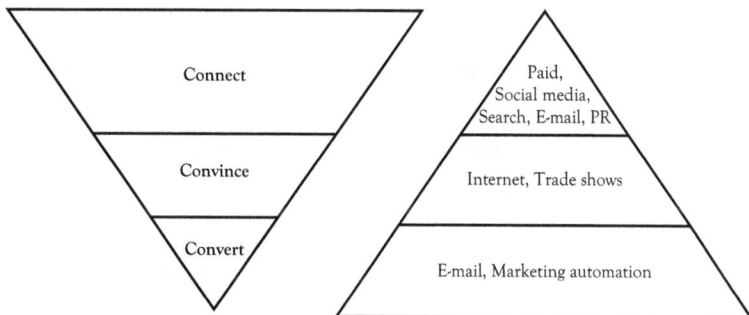

Figure 8.2 Media specialists should be looking for ways to achieve the three objectives in the left pyramid by choosing media tactics from the tactics listed on the right

And don't forget earned media, especially PR. Placing articles in key publications and websites, and the attendant third-party endorsement of editors and industry gatekeepers is very important in building credibility.

You'll want to select the tactics best suited for each stage of that process:

- **Media preferences.** Do the members of your target audience have any particular favorites? Do you know the best places to reach them?
- **Frequency.** It's advertising lore that a prospect needs to see a message seven times before it makes an impression. And while that number is often debated, one thing is certain: You can't really count on a single exposure to break through all the clutter. You'll need to be thinking about increasing the likelihood that the message gets through and resonates.

Overall, you'll need to weigh the strengths of each medium and the unique roles they could play in your campaign.

Map

The mapping step plays an important role in the integration of the campaign. It is where you will decide how the campaign is supposed to work. When you determine what happens at each step. And how you will deliver the outcomes you are expected to achieve.

You'll start by reconvening the team in a room with ample white board space. Then you'll ask the media and creative groups to present their work. You can have them present separately but it's best, though, if they're working together already, to have them present jointly, continuing to break down silos and build a campaign.

At the meeting, and preferably before, the creative and media teams should be talking about how each medium that is selected is appropriate for this client, product, and campaign. The most important step is deciding what role you'd like each medium to play. And ultimately finalize a map of the campaign and call out how it is to work, how it will produce the desired outcome.

Assign each tactic to a stage in the Connect–Convince–Convert model shown in Figure 8.3.

Start with the Connect phase.

Connect

From the model, we already know that paid placements and search tactics will go in the Connect phase. The creative team should present its connect concepts while the media team should explain which media options will perform the best for the specific application.

Place the recommendations on the Connect–Convince–Convert pyramid, as shown in Figure 8.4.

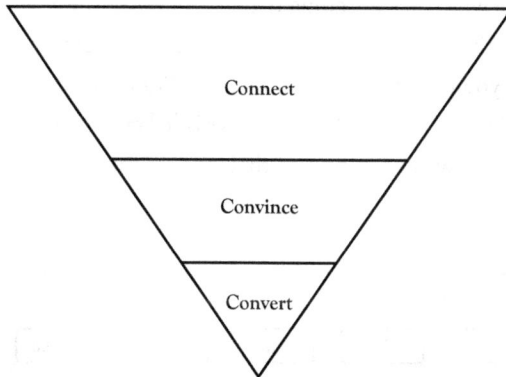

Figure 8.3 The Connect–Convince–Convert model

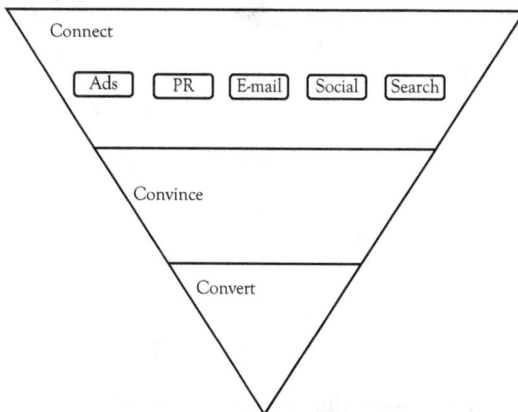

Figure 8.4 Media recommendations for the Connect phase

Even better if you can include a headline and maybe even a sketch (as in Figure 8.5), to give everyone a feel for what the entire program for a new dogfood might look like.

You'll want to begin thinking about your expected outcomes at each stage. Make sure each tactic has a strong call-to-action, connecting to the next step in the process outlined in Connect–Convince–Convert.

We're showing a landing page in Figure 8.6, but it could just as easily be an event like a trade show or sale.

There could also be separate landing pages for each tactic, as shown in Figure 8.7.

A key point: Your call to action is not simply "click here," especially for the attract media. The stronger the offer, the better. You'll want to tell your audience what they are going to get if they take the action you're recommending. Show them how they are going to benefit, as an incentive. For example, you might say something like, "Watch a video of the ACME ABC widget in action." Or, "Hear what satisfied customers say about how the MEGA XYZ Widget improved their car's performance."

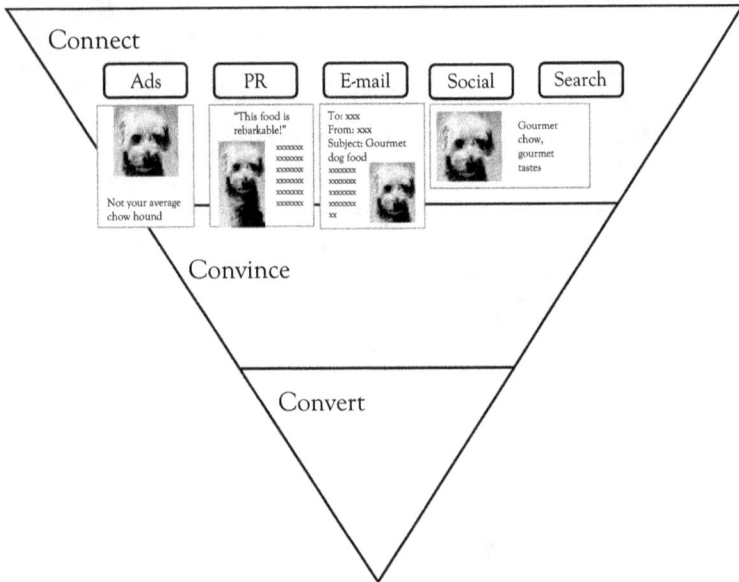

Figure 8.5 A slightly more illustrative example shows Connect tactics with a little more creative detail

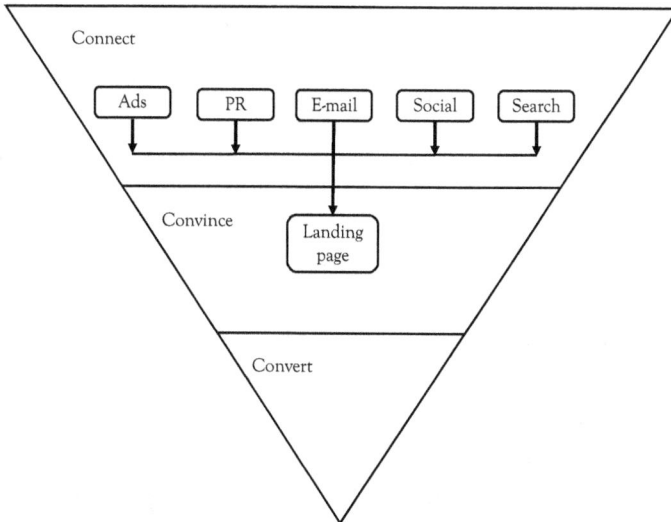

Figure 8.6 A campaign with a single landing page

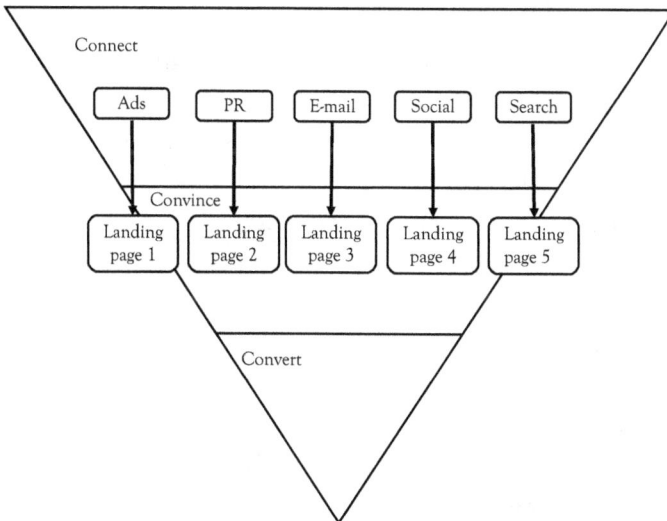

Figure 8.7 A campaign with separate landing pages for each tactic

Usually, but not always, you'll be promoting the anchor content in the call to action. That's the most persuasive piece of content you have for the first round of your program. Don't be afraid to promote the same piece of content in all the different media. In fact, you should keep the anchor content the same until you are at the point where you are testing an alternative call to action, which usually happens later in the campaign. You can, of course, change the call-to-action phrasing.

Convince

The goal of the Convince phase, of course, is to get your prospects to take an action that gets them in your orbit—filling out a form, requesting a sales call, visiting a tradeshow booth, or otherwise raising their hand to indicate interest and a desire to go further.

It usually requires some anchor content, an attractive communication that you can promote heavily in the Connect phase. You may or may not want to gate that content. But the goal of the Convince stage is to get a prospect to identify themselves, one way or another.

A Note About Gating Content

A recent study[2] found that 25 percent of B2B marketers often gate content, 34 percent sometimes do, and 5 percent do so all of the time. As Ray Schultz wrote in *MediaPost*,[3] that's way too much.

Content gating has been around almost since the beginning of the Internet. I sat in one meeting where an aggressive marketer wanted to gate *all* of his company's web content. And I've seen many occasions where it was routine to do so, even for information such as data sheets or product catalogs.

In one outstanding example, a client launched an aggressive e-mail campaign that promised the recipient a white paper addressing an industry issue, then linked them right to a form with about 20 fields. The theory was, all the company had to do was sit back and watch the leads roll in.

---

[2] Finite and 93x. 2020. "The B2B Content Marketing Report," https://finite. cogniclick.app/report/12884cab7

[3] R. Schultz. 2020. "The Gate Swings Both Ways: Don't Make It Too Hard To Access B2B Content," *MediaPost*. www.mediapost.com/publications/article/357436/the-gate-swings-both-ways-dont-make-it-too-hard.html.

They sat back, all right. Because nothing happened. The program landed with a dull thud. It didn't help that most of the campaign read like a college research paper.

Many others feel the same way. Multiple source quote David Meerman Scott's estimate that users download ungated content 20 to 50 times more often than gated content.

Leads Are Good. But…

I get it. Everyone wants leads. But the marketers mentioned previously were missing an important point: no one wants to cough up their information *gratis*. They want something in return.

Data sheets aren't enough. Most people expect to get them without registration. And for good reason: *your company benefits every time someone downloads those data sheets.* And if you don't give them that information without conditions, perhaps a competitor will.

What sense does it make to penalize your audience by requiring that they register when *you want them to have it?*

Compared to the old, pre-Internet days, when you had to fill out a response card and wait six weeks for printed materials to arrive, today's instant downloads are a bonanza for marketers. No printing, no postage, no handling costs. The prospect downloads the data using their equipment and their printers (if they go that far). All in real time. All at their expense.

Why in any sane universe would you want to discourage or dissuade them from doing that?

Are you even pretending that these materials contain something your competitors will want to know? As if they don't have your data sheets already?

The same is true of case histories. Heck, we write them up and send them to publications and websites *for free*. Because we want them to use them. Distribute them. Send them everywhere in the known universe.

It's even true of white papers, which I define as position papers on key technology topics, written from your company's perspective.

Once again, why in the world would you think they are proprietary? And don't you want all your prospects and customers to have free access to that information?

Gating Requires Unique Value

To me, content that is gated must have some kind of unique value.

It either needs to contain proprietary research, developed at your company's expense and illuminating a key development (usually technology) that your prospect or customer will benefit from. Act on. Use to enhance or improve their product or service offering.

Or it needs to have proprietary product information. Computer-aided design (CAD) drawings for design engineers. Or Revit files for architects.

Other than that, as they said in the early days of the Internet, information wants to be free.

I get it. Everyone wants leads. But by putting your needs ahead of theirs, you're making your problem their problem. That's not a good look. And not a great way to start a relationship.

My golden rule for gating? Give first. Before you get the lead.

At the point where they complete a form and identify themselves, they are a lead, but just at the beginning stages. Are they really a prospect? Do they really want or need what you have to sell? Someone who is ready to buy, of course, then becomes an SQL, assuming they meet any other qualifications that your sales management team requests (like coming from a certain industry or company). Sales may insist, for instance, that only leads from a targeted list of companies are qualified.

Determining whether a contact is worth pursuing is where the marketers have to coordinate with their company's sales leadership. Establishing the lead qualification criteria requires close coordination between marketing and sales and goes a long way in closing the gap between the two. It requires negotiation and good communication—striking a balance between "no leads" and "these leads are crap."

That's become increasingly important because of the increased demand for your reps' time. A lukewarm lead that once may have been followed up by a sales rep may no longer be considered worth the time, as reps are under increasing pressure to sell quickly and move onto the next prospect.

Unfortunately, in most cases, leads aren't ready for sales follow-up at that point. And, as a result, marketing needs to continue to nurture them, providing them more information to build their sales readiness. That's where the final stage of the process, Convert, comes in.

Convert

The team's goal in the Convert phase is to find that last "closer," the last bit of evidence or proof the prospect might need to make them ready to buy. What we said about having a compelling piece of anchor content in the Convince state does not, however, imply that it is the *only* important piece of content in the program. Back in the bad old days, one solid piece of content may have been enough. But no more. With marketing holding onto and nurturing qualified leads until they are ready for sales, you'll need some even bigger and better content pieces to aid in the conversion step.

For instance, the "anchor" for the Connect stage might be a white paper reviewing the latest developments in your particular technology. Now what?

That's where closer content comes in. Perhaps you create a video interview with one of your top researchers. Maybe it's a testimonial or case history. Or a calculator to estimate savings. The point is, now that you have a marketing qualified lead, you need to up your game and create even better content to close the deal (as shown in Figure 8.8). The more compelling the piece, the greater the likelihood of conversion.

Some companies rely on marketing automation for this stage. Unfortunately, many of them view the technology as a form of magic, a way to keep hounding people until they are ready to convert. That's not the best use of the technology and may antagonize more people than it converts.

Remember, what's automated is only the physical process of reaching out to the prospect. A human being still has to define and create the content that will entice the lead to convert. Admittedly, that may differ from

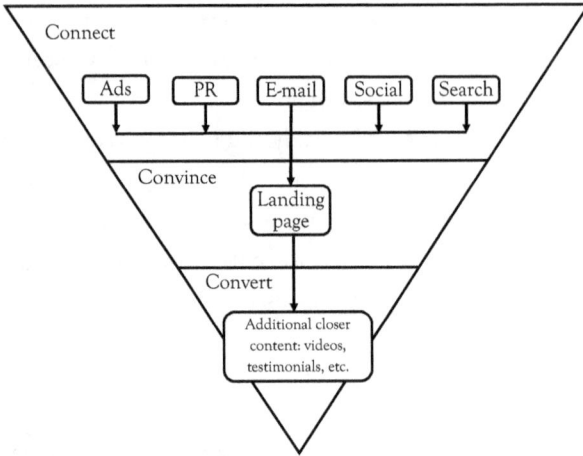

Figure 8.8 You need really compelling content at the Convert stage to close the deal

one prospect to another. So your task is to gather enough information about each prospect and learn enough about your audience that you have a good idea whether they will be swayed by a calculator, a testimonial, a research study, or some other piece of premium content.

Your goal is to outline a plan and a rationale for reaching out to people and offering them something of value—usually more concrete information about how they might benefit from your product. So at this point, the goal of the team will be to answer the question, what will you offer a lukewarm, qualified lead who is not ready to buy?

One final consideration is testing. Are there approaches, concepts, or hypotheses you would like to evaluate as alternatives? If so, make sure to structure this research into your campaign. And evaluate at appropriate points of the process. *More on this in the next chapter.*

Create

Following the process, develop materials following the messaging platform and the approved creative concept. Unfortunately, this is one step that often suffers in the typical crush to be more productive with assignments on individual tactics coming through under separate projects or work orders.

To be most effective, all the tactics in a campaign should be created together. That means written together, laid out together, reviewed together, and approved together. That's the best way to get everyone to think of the campaign as a unified package. And the only way to make sure you haven't missed something. Because, in my experience, you will.

They should be reviewed as a group with all the reviewers looking at the finished campaign map to ensure everything is working as planned. All the creative, all the media plans, reviewed together, as a package.

The materials should go to the client or technical reviewers in the same way and the account manager or marketing manager should walk the reviewers through the entire campaign to make sure they understand how it will work. The idea is to encourage everyone to see the campaign from the 20,000-foot level, before they dive into the tactics.

And while this may seem cumbersome, consider the current practice in most companies, with all the tactics coming through separately. One by one. Disconnected. Not integrated. No wonder these programs don't produce leads. And people draw the conclusion that marketing is not working. The only thing that's not working is disconnected-tactics marketing. That never will work. And never did.

Produce and Launch

Before the individual pieces go out together, I'd encourage you to take one more look at them as a whole. Walking through the campaign with the entire team. I'd physically point to the call to action on each tactic, making sure it connects to the next step in the process. Ask your team these questions:

- What is this?
- What happens next?
- What level of response are we expecting?
- How will we measure?
- When will we know if these tactics are working?
- When can we review?

And pay specific attention to the anchor, closer, and nurturing content, making sure they're working properly.

After the campaign is launched, you'll want to have your team call up all the pieces to make sure links are working and that the entire campaign is functioning the way it should. Walk through it just like a customer would.

Working With an Agency

As someone who spent a large portion of his working career in an advertising agency, I would be remiss if I did not offer a few observations about how to get the best results in working with one. There are a few basic principles you'd want to follow.

Agree on the strategy. I'm a great believer in not only having a brief for the creative team, but having the brief signed off by the client before anyone lifts a pencil (or mouse).

Identify the decision makers. Clients could save themselves a ton of money, if they decided who the final decision maker was and had that person involved from the outset—approving the brief, picking the concept to develop, going to a video shoot, approving the final work. If it's the marketing manager, great. If it's the CEO, that's fine too. But have them in from the beginning.

Build in measurement. The brief needs to define what success looks like, what the key performance indicators are.

No heroes. The first agency I worked at recognized that, sometimes, the chemistry is not right. If the account manager and the client contact are not in sync, it's going to be a nightmare for everyone. That may also extend to other client-facing players like the creative director and the strategist. In fact, I'd recommend swapping out strategists on a regular basis, say two years, because they tend to wear out their welcome after a while. The reason? Strategists get tired of saying "no" as quickly as client-side people get tired of hearing it. When you swap out the strategist, at least the client starts to hear it in a different voice.

Chapter Summary

Points to Remember

- Planning a marketing campaign is like being an orchestra conductor.
- The process harnesses a wide range of personalities and skills.
- It follows a seven-step process from planning through optimization and reporting.

Advancing Brand Vision

By following the integration process outlined previously, we tie the campaign to the business strategy. And, by organizing and integrating marketing tactics, campaigns advance *Brand Vision* and the goal of making sure marketing is as effective as possible. And, as we shall see in Chapter 9, they make measurement and accountability possible.

Next, we learn how to optimize marketing campaigns.

PART V

Measurement: Analytics That Illuminate

The preceding four parts of the *Brand Vision* process have painstakingly built that clear line of sight between business strategy and marketing tactics. Step by step, we've discussed strategy, the audience, messaging, and campaigns.

But it's the final stage of the process, measurement, where the process really pays off for marketers.

First, by giving you the tools to optimize your campaigns, *Brand Vision* allows you to continuously improve both the quality of your campaign and the results it achieves. The goal of posting quickly, then making adjustments on the fly gives you the agility that's often been lacking.

And second, by helping you determine the return on your company's marketing investment, *Brand Vision* allows you to demonstrate that marketing can be both tactical and strategic. Not an optional expense but a necessary investment. A manufacturing input as valid as energy or raw materials.

Marketing then becomes a data-driven partner that can not only look back to a marketing success but also a strategic resource that can look to the future and predict likely outcomes for the company's next big initiative.

CHAPTER 9

Optimization

Chapter Overview

For years, marketers have struggled to take advantage of all the capabilities digital marketing offers. All too often they are inundated by the reams of data their efforts generate. But, by organizing the various tactics into campaigns, marketers can achieve the continuous improvement that business executives expect from other parts of the enterprise, especially manufacturing. The result is better performance for their marketing efforts and greater value for the company.

Putting All That Data to Use

Despite protestations to the contrary, most marketers really don't optimize their marketing programs and tactics. First, it's notoriously difficult. Second, as noted earlier, most companies haven't set up their marketing initiatives in easy-to-evaluate packages like campaigns. Third, creatives all too often don't like having their art evaluated using criteria other than aesthetic appeal. And fourth, marketing managers have successfully resisted scrutiny for decades. And are not giving up that position without a fight.

As a result, marketers generally adopt a fix-it-and-forget-it attitude—once a campaign goes out the door, it belongs to the ages, never to return. That approach simply won't fly anymore. The digital revolution has brought all kinds of data collection and measurability capabilities to communications. Business execs are demanding the level of accountability they get from all other areas of the enterprise. Marketers are being pressured to use the enormous amounts of data these activities generate to improve the performance of their systems and demonstrate return on marketing investment.

Why Not Optimize at the Tactical Level?

As mentioned in Chapter 7, tactics don't generate leads and sales. Only campaigns do that. And recent experience has shown that disconnected tactics are a miserable failure. A tragic waste of money. And that by integrating tactics into campaigns, markets can provide greater value for their companies.

It's not easy. But, with practice, it will come. Here's how to get started.

First, Keep Your Cool

By assigning every tactic to a level of the Connect–Convince–Convert model, *Brand Vision* campaigns are designed to enable easy optimization. You can go tactic by tactic and see if it is meeting the goals of that particular stage (note that we're only talking about the goals of the stage, not the campaign's goals). Identify the techniques that are working and extend the most effective headlines, offers, or copy to the other parts of the program. That way, you can focus more effort on the tactics that need your attention the most.

Are your Connect mechanisms working, generating enough traffic to your landing page or trade show booth? If so, is your landing page getting the kinds of responses you were hoping for? Are prospects downloading the spec sheets, viewing the videos, and scrolling down the page? And are they taking that next step, becoming a SQL?

All too often, marketers are afraid to ask themselves tough questions like these. But that's the best way to improve. And learn how to do even better the next time around. In the past, "No" answers to these questions were problems. But not anymore. Rather, they are opportunities—chances to replace something that's not working. And improve your results.

You're building a marketing machine. And most businesspeople understand that machines have to be maintained. New products have to be tested and retested. Systems have to be tweaked, optimized. That's continuous improvement, what lean manufacturing advocates call *kaizen*. And that's the role of the optimization stage.

Then, Make Sure All the Parts Are Working

As soon as the program is up and running, you'll want to ask your entire team to check and make sure everything is working properly. Are there any broken links? Are all the media running properly and in the right place? Are the analytics set up properly?

Reconvene the Team

When you start getting enough data to make analysis worthwhile, the next step is getting the team together and running through the program. Ask everyone to describe any changes they identified and made.

Then look at the flow chart. The Connect–Convince–Convert model was designed with a graphical representation of the results in mind. Since each stage has a consistent call to action, the Key Performance Indicator (KPI) for that stage measures the campaign's success in getting the prospect to complete that action:

- **Impressions**—measures the number of people exposed to the campaign.
- **Visits**—tracks the number of times a prospect comes to the landing page from one of the *Connect* tactics.
- **Form completions**—lists the number of prospects who break anonymity and provide their contact information in the *Convince* stage.
- **Leads/sales**—counts the number of prospects in the *Convert* stage who become SQLs or actually make a purchase.

The arrows on the right (as shown in Figure 9.1) give you a quick reference showing at a glance what's working and what's not. Let's call this WW/WN.

After reviewing the results, you'll want to talk about the flow of the campaign. Is the paid media performing as expected? What is generating the most traffic to your destination (generally your web landing page but could be your trade show booth)? And are those visitors converting at

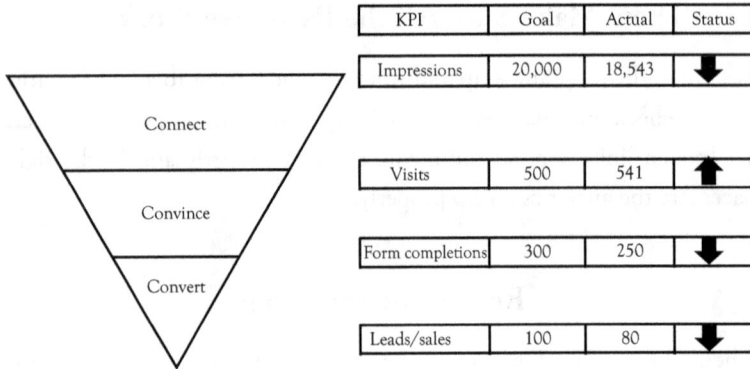

KPI	Goal	Actual	Status
Impressions	20,000	18,543	⬇
Visits	500	541	⬆
Form completions	300	250	⬇
Leads/sales	100	80	⬇

Figure 9.1 The Connect–Convince–Convert model helps you see very quickly what's working and what's not

the same rate—you obviously don't want to optimize for a tactic that is generating traffic that doesn't convert.

The media specialists can really help the creative team understand the data. Not simply that this ad didn't work. But more likely, this headline worked in paid search but not in paid media placements. And then, as a group, the team can figure out why.

Admittedly, your media specialists could simply adjust the campaign, according to what's working. And many companies do that. But that misses a huge opportunity to help the entire team get a better understanding of what works in each medium. To help everyone learn more about the audience. And to come up with better solutions. Solutions that retain or even enhance the creative concept or rely on deeper strategic insights.

You'll want to capture all these observations and insights on a white board as shown in Table 9.1.

Table 9.1 Use a white board to capture the team's observations

What's Working	What's Not?
Paid search	Paid media
Organic search	Landing page
Public relations release	Anchor content
	E-mail

Revisions in Several Rounds

You'll want to attack the revision cycle in several stages or rounds, going for the quick wins first. That shows progress that will make everyone feel good.

Round One

To make the best use of available resources, you'll want to scale up what's working and scale back what's not. If paid search is working, for instance, make sure you're spending at least the amount you've budgeted, and maybe shift some additional cash from any tactics that aren't performing. And delete the ads and paid search creative that is performing poorly, boosting the top ads and the overall performance of the program. That will provide additional data about the program.

But be careful, especially about extending your conclusions to an entire category of media. In one case several years ago, a client cut its print advertising, figuring there would be minimal impact on the program, since few leads were coming in using the vanity URL. When we stopped the ads, we noticed a significant drop in organic search traffic a short time later. And the volume returned after the ads resumed. So something might not look as if it's working, but it might be delivering value in a way that you simply weren't anticipating or that wasn't easy to measure. That is what makes campaign development an art form all on its own.

The team should agree on what all of these changes are and schedule them for implementation as soon as possible. The media specialists should share the results of these upgrades as soon as sufficient data has been gathered.

Round Two

Next, you'll want to talk about any obvious fixes, based on the observations your team made in the meetings.

For creatives, that means taking another look at the finished pieces. Focus on the key points:

- Call to action: Is it prominent and easy to see? Does it make a strong offer: either implying a benefit or promising critical information?

- Are the heads and visuals clear and compelling? Do they promise a benefit and/or address a pain point?
- Are the key pieces of content, especially the anchor content, effective? Do they actually deliver the benefits you promise? Are there minor edits or tweaks that might make them work better or make it easier to get the main point of the piece?

Next, you should review the campaign structure, to see if any of these elements are holding you back:

- Forms: Are the response mechanisms too complex? All too often, marketers try to capture all the information they need in the first contact (as shown in Figure 9.2). That's really too much to ask. Some experts estimate the response rate declines by 20 percent for each question after the third one.

The CCC program mentioned at the end of the last chapter was a great example. In compliance with corporate requirements, the response

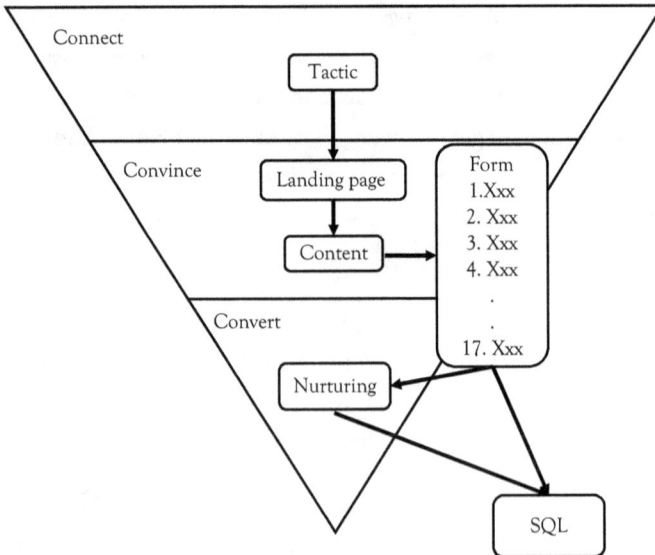

Figure 9.2 *Many companies scare prospects away by asking for too much information in an initial contact form*

form required the prospect to complete the standard contact form—all 17 lines including name, mailing address, company name, industry, birth sign, pet's name, eye color, weight, and favorite rock band. (Just kidding about those last few). Not surprisingly, we got very few leads in the first week. I asked the company how it was handling the leads when they came in and found that, despite the lengthy form, a customer service rep still had to call every customer to obtain the information needed to config- ure the product. As a result, we slashed the contact form to three lines: name, company, and phone number, figuring the rep would gather the additional information during the call. I wanted the process to be simple. Easy. And leads immediately started flowing in.

- Firewalls. Many marketers want to force customers to give up their anonymity and provide contact information before they give them access to the anchor content (as shown in Figure 9.3).

Conceivably, if you are an industry leader and you're promising a powerful specification tool or research study, it might work. But I have seen that tried several times and never have seen it produce more than a trickle of leads. In fact, for one client, we had an apples-to-apples

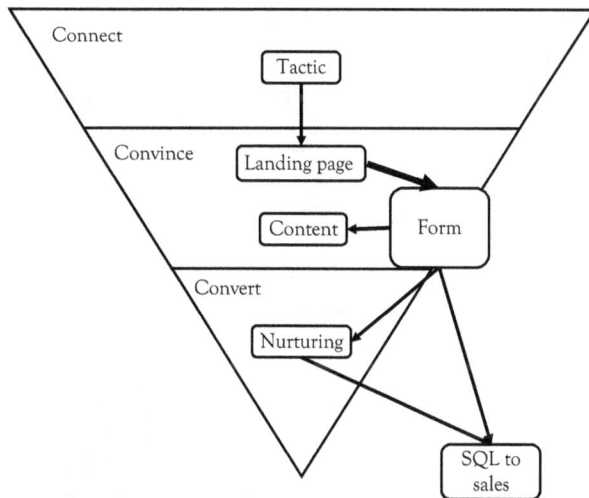

Figure 9.3 One program I worked on made prospects fill out a form before they got the content. It received almost no leads

comparison, with one division offering a free white paper and another requiring registration. The protected content not only got few leads, but the information critical to the success of the business unit was seen by only a handful of people. With the free content, on the other hand, many prospects downloaded the white paper and were intrigued enough that they voluntarily filled out a request form to know more about how the technology or product in question might help them. And that program shown in Figure 9.4, got a lot of valuable leads. As a result, I think the trust we show prospects generally pays off, so include me in the "information wants to be free" crowd.

- Qualification criteria. As noted in Chapter 4, some companies are being very aggressive with the time sales reps spend with prospects. They require that a lead meet a number of criteria before it is accepted by ready sales. For instance, the prospect needs to come from a targeted company. Or be planning to buy within 90 days. Often, both. The tighter

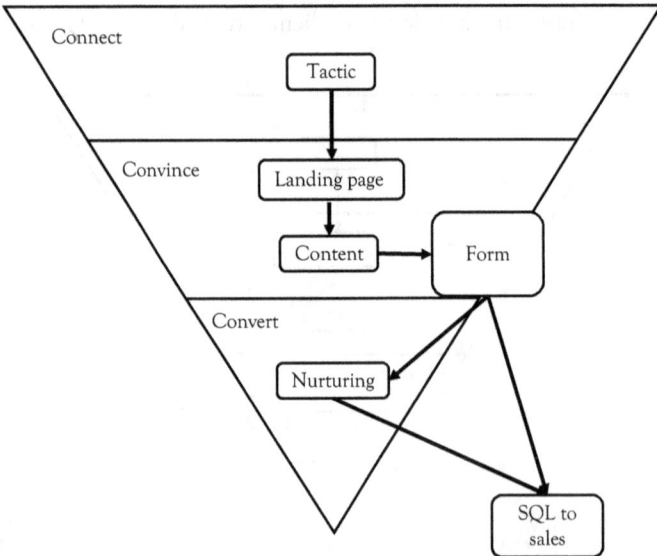

Figure 9.4 *Meanwhile, a similar program for the same client did very well by giving the prospect access to the content, then including a lead form for those who wanted to know more*

the criteria, of course, the fewer leads will qualify. But these criteria can only be changed in consultation with sales management. Lest you be accused of providing the "crap" leads referred to in Chapter 8.

After you've identified these actions, you'll conclude your meeting of the team by agreeing to a schedule for these updates, so they're not all happening at once. Ideally, by doing the upgrade in stages, you'll have a better idea what's working and what's not. Unfortunately, that's all too often not the real world we live in. You may have to make two major changes simultaneously—for instance, a stronger call to action on the paid ads, combined with improvements in the anchor content on a landing page. Not perfect, because the landing page improvements invariably will impact the paid media's conversion rate. But often, time is of the essence.

And have your media specialists notify the team about the changes made in their area, so that everyone has a good handle on the progress you're making.

Later Rounds of Revisions

If none of these techniques work and you're still not achieving the objectives you laid out at the start of the project, it's probably time to go back to your basic assumptions.

In creative, you'll want to take a look at your concept. Does it connect with the target audience? Or is it too abstract? And is the anchor content truly definitive? Is it helping or hindering the sale? Look especially at the tactics that are working, for clues.

You also may need to take another look at your strategy. Is the core idea correct? What about the pain points? Have you identified the right audience? One telling indication that you haven't would be that sales reps following up on leads are being referred to someone else in the organization. An indication that the person you thought was the decision maker is deferring to another player on the team.

And has the competitive landscape changed, altering the uniqueness of your position?

Admittedly, that feels as if you're starting all over again. And, in some ways, you are. But it's not the same. You're smarter. You know at least one approach that didn't work, and maybe you have some idea why.

Better, you find that out sooner than later. Especially before your boss or client figures it out.

Optimization Is Field Testing

Optimization gives you a chance for a shakedown cruise or trial run. You'll want to take advantage of the opportunity to maximize the success of your program and use available resources more wisely.

The goal is to have an optimized, fully functioning campaign field-tested and producing leads or sales. With the cost of maintaining the program viewed as almost a manufacturing input rather than an expense.

The program can run for months or even years, raising the expenditure level up and down as needed to sustain your level of production. And it can continue to operate until you have an optimized, fully functioning campaign that is field-tested and ready to take its place.

For more on optimizing marketing spending, see Sunil Gupta's book, *Driving Digital Strategy: A Guide to Reimagining Your Business, 9. Measuring and Optimizing Marketing Spend.*[1]

Chapter Summary

Points to Remember

- Often inundated with data, marketers have struggled to take advantages of the capabilities digital marketing offers.
- By organizing tactics into campaigns, marketers can provide greater value.
- Optimization is like field testing, allowing you to improve campaign performance.

---

[1] S. Gupta. 2018. *Driving Digital Strategy: A Guide to Reimagining Your Business, 9. Measuring and Optimizing Marketing Spend.* Boston, MA: Harvard Business Press Books.

Advancing Brand Vision

The optimization process provides yet another chance to make sure concepts, media selections, and campaign structures are aligned with the corporate strategy. And, even more importantly, it helps marketers improve the performance of their strategically driven campaigns.

Next, we bring it all together with analytics and measurement that shows the company the return on its marketing investment.

CHAPTER 10

Return on Investment

Chapter Overview

Top management has long demanded greater accountability from market-ing. But calculating ROI is an elusive goal, fraught with a wide range of challenges. Knowing what works in marketing, however, is a game-changer, allowing marketers to move from being an expense to being a critical input. And perhaps even earning marketing a seat at the table. We'll also see how to develop an ROI report C-level execs will understand and appreciate.

Seizing a Priceless Opportunity

A few years ago, the client who originally launched this inquiry link-ing business strategy and marketing tactics was introducing one of its signature pieces of construction equipment at a huge trade show. We supported the effort with a full marketing effort, including advertising, public relations, e-mail, video, and social media. And, of course, there were the expected trade show displays and graphics.

The program was a big success, with the company selling all the mod-els it had in stock, as well as all the products it would be able to make for the next year.

I recognized very quickly that the successful launch was an opportu-nity to calculate the marketing ROI from the program. We compiled all the costs we had incurred for the show. And though we didn't have sales figures, we could easily multiply the number of units sold by the sticker price to get a reasonably close revenue estimate.

Admittedly, it wasn't perfect. Other products were promoted at the show, of course. And like any other trade marketing event, it offered a host of additional opportunities to build brand recognition and industry stature.

So, the costs were probably overstated and the sales were understated. But the return on marketing investment still was nearly 20 to 1. The benefit of knowing that? Priceless.

An Elusive Goal

Calculating ROI for marketing expenditures has always been an elusive goal. Retail giant John Wanamaker famously remarked that "Half the money I spend on advertising is wasted; the trouble is, I don't know which half."

There are a number of reasons for this indecision. Depending on whom you are talking to, calculating ROI is either difficult, if not impossible. Or it's a piece of cake. Here's both sides.

ROI Is Hard

Here's why ROI is such a challenge:

- **Technology barriers.** To determine marketing ROI, you need information from across the enterprise, tapping into web analytics, sales management, or customer relationship management (CRM) software, and accounting systems, at the very least. Good luck breaking down those silos.
- **Turf wars.** If you think those technical systems have trouble talking to each other, imagine the gulf between the humans who use them.
- **Sales-marketing alignment.** First and foremost among the turf wars is the Mars–Venus relationship between sales and marketing. With "who gets credit for the sale" being a familiar refrain. And alternately, "These leads are crap" and "We're not getting any leads," referred to in Chapter 8. There seem to be more than enough reasons for the two camps to eye each other with skepticism.
- **Intangibles.** As noted previously (and throughout this work), marketing deals with a host of intangibles. Like brand identity and preference. And buyer behavior that is difficult to predict.

- **Channels.** Add in outside partners like distributors and you have an even more complex nut to crack.
- **Attribution.** What if someone sees an ad, visits a web page, watches a video, downloads a brochure, responds to an e-mail, and finally buys a product? Which tactic gets credit (that idea again) for the sale? And Heaven forbid if the sale happens through a channel.
- **Long sales cycles.** Even some consumer products (such as appliances, cars, and houses) have long sales cycles, making it more difficult to keep track of whether or if a sale takes place.

No, ROI Is Easy

On the other hand, ROI can be incredibly simply, as sharp-eyed chief financial officers (CFOs) have been pointing out for decades. The company spends $300,000 to go to a trade show and gets 100 sales leads. That's $3,000 a lead. Simple, straightforward, just what you'd expect from a CFO.

But that oversimplifies the issue, marketers quickly respond. It fails to account for the broader benefits of a trade show appearance, such as name recognition, audience awareness, and industry stature and presence.

And, more importantly, it fails to account for ongoing efforts such as branding, social media, public relations, e-mail, and website development that are not part of a discrete event like a trade show. But play an important role in lead generation, product promotion, and market penetration.

As a result, evaluating the impact of marketing is an ongoing struggle, as C-level executives demand to know how their marketing dollars are spent. And what they're getting for their money.

The Benefits Are Game-Changing

Despite the problems mentioned previously, it's well worth your time to do the math. ROI isn't simply another "nice to have." Knowing what works in marketing is a game changer, both for marketers and their companies.

For marketers, knowing what works and what doesn't changes how marketing is perceived. It's no longer an expense. One that can be cut at the first sign of economic troubles. And it changes the perception of marketers as well, earning them a seat at the table when important decisions are made.

For the company, imagine that they know the answer to Wanamaker's challenge. That they know what it will cost to bring products to market or penetrate new industries. With predictable results and knowable costs. Think of the competitive advantage that confers.

The alternative for marketing is not pretty. Without ROI, marketing will continue to be marginalized, with slightly higher perceived value than the company bowling team. Perhaps not as much as a lobby renovation. If we can't change that dynamic, we're doomed. Headed for the scrap heap of history. And we should be.

Brand Vision is dedicated to changing that. It's about creating a clear line of sight between business strategy and marketing tactics that will demonstrate what's at stake in marketing. And how the company benefits.

How Do You Do That, With All the Obstacles Mentioned Earlier?

If you have the sales figures, it's a relatively straightforward proposition:

$$\frac{\text{Sales totals}}{\text{Marketing expenses}} = \text{Marketing return on investment}$$

Unfortunately, it's not that simple. Most companies have a number of obstacles, such as corporate silos, distributor relationships, or sales silos, that stand in the way. There is an alternative, however, if you don't have actual sales figures.

No Sales Data? No Problem

A consistent problem in many companies is that there isn't dependable sales data. Maybe the company has a long sales cycle. Or it sells through distribution. Or the technical silos are just too high.

There is an alternative, if you have just a few pieces of data:

- The number of SQLs you send to your sales reps;
- Sales conversion rate for SQLs;
- Customer lifetime value (CLV).

Most organizations have this data readily available. Marketing will normally have the number of leads. The sales conversion rate usually comes from the sales department. And the CLV figure, advanced by Roland T. Rust, Christine Moorman, and Gaurav Bhalla,[1] should be available from your CRM system.

Then it's simply a matter of multiplying the number of leads from your campaign or program times the conversion rate to get the number of likely sales from the initiative. Then multiply the number of likely sales times the lifetime customer value to get the expected return on your marketing investment.

Number of SQLs × sales conversion rate × lifetime value of a customer = Expected revenue

To get the ROI, you'll simply need to divide that expected revenue by the total marketing expenditure.

Expected revenue / Marketing expenditure = ROI

Is that perfect? No. But it's better than allowing marketing to be held hostage by other functions. It allows you to begin the conversation, showing you're serious about ROI. And you'll be surprised how rapidly the discussion changes when you're talking about real money.

[1] R.T. Roland, C. Moorman, and G. Bhalla. 2010. "Rethinking Marketing," In *HBR's 10 Must Reads on Strategic Marketing (with featured article "Marketing Myopia," by Theodore Levitt)*, 6. Boston: Harvard Business Review Press. Kindle Edition.

A Note to Analytics People About the Pursuit of Perfection

Yes, my analytic friends, marketing statistics are rarely going to be perfect. I get that. But we have to start somewhere. Time is a-wasting. We need to do something, *anything*. Because if you wait for the perfect time, it will never come. As noted here, you may not know the exact status of all the leads or the sales that resulted from a campaign. But if you know the raw leads, the conversion rate, and the CLV, you have *something*.

And that's a start, until you get something better. And you will. Executives who see an honest effort (and want more) will find the money to get better tools and the tracking you need.

Conversely, if you keep saying, "we can't give you anything," top brass will think you're not serious. And that you really don't want to measure the outcomes of marketing campaigns. That's not a place you want to be.

In his book, *The Heart of Business: Leadership Principles for the Next Era of Capitalism*, Hubert Joly talks about his own struggles with "the quest for perfection." Something I'd encourage all marketing analytics professionals to take to heart.

Reporting ROI to Management

Like the tree falling in the proverbial forest, a marketing ROI calculation is only valuable if it's seen. As a result, an ROI report should be distributed to top management for the following reasons:

- To show the benefit of marketing;
- To demonstrate that the program went through an optimization process (not unlike product development or manufacturing) that explored all avenues and logical alternatives until the campaign was delivering maximum benefit to the company;
- To prove that marketing is a good steward of corporate expenditures;

- To document that learning took place and was captured and preserved;
- To show that the negative findings were captured to avoid repetition in the future and build on the positive outcomes that occurred, guiding future marketing campaigns;
- To put marketing in a position to predict what benefits the corporation will achieve by extending the campaign in question; applying the *Brand Vision* approach to other marketing efforts; or launching new campaigns in support of new products, market-expansion initiatives or even branding.

As mentioned in Chapter 7, we do not recommend talking about individual tactics. Because each tactic plays a unique role in a campaign, isolating the impact of an individual element is likely to lead to confusion. For example, everyone acknowledges that trade shows score highly in lead quantity and quality. But focusing on the success of shows misses the value of the rest of the program that actually delivered prospects to your booth. Not just the space ads, e-mails, and web landing pages that created traffic, but also the years of brand building (through public relations, advertising, and social media) that burned your company's name into their brains and had prospects looking for you at the show.

The point is that the tactics in your program should each have an intended purpose. Some, like the show, with its one-on-one contact, are exquisitely designed to convert live prospects. Others, such as ads, e-mail, and websites, are designed to connect with, convince, and cultivate those prospects until they're ready.

Building a Clear Line of Sight

We've outlined a variety of tools thus far. And we're ready to combine them to build that line of sight between business strategy and marketing tactics.

Here's how a *Brand Vision* ROI report is structured to clearly demonstrate the clear line of sight you've created between business strategy and marketing tactics.

First, Who Are You?

You'll want to begin with your business strategy (shown in Figure 10.1). You'll want to state clearly whether your company's market discipline and differentiation, to use the Treacy–Wiersma formulation outlined in Part I, is primarily product leadership, operational excellence, or customer intimacy. Or something else, if you are using one of the other business models.

Then, you'll connect with the business objectives (described in Chapter 2). This shows top management you're paying attention and are thinking strategically. You're working as hard as they are to advance your company's business plan (shown in Figure 10.2).

So the combined business strategy and business objectives pyramid goes right at the top of the ROI report (shown in Figure 10.3). That will give your managers the strategic context for your marketing initiative.

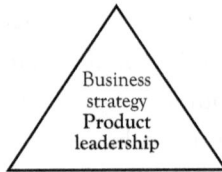

Figure 10.1 Begin with the business strategy

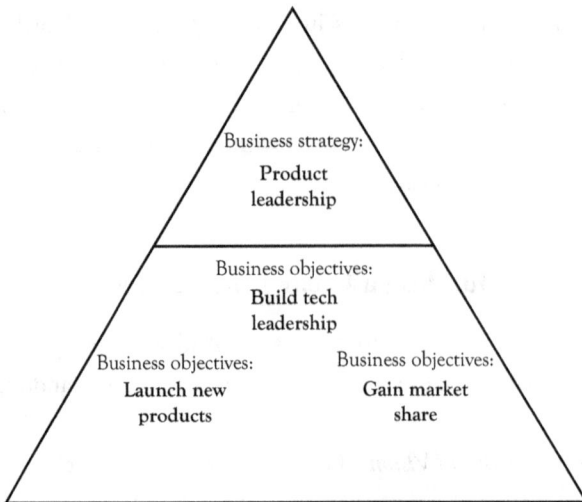

Figure 10.2 Next, add in the business objectives

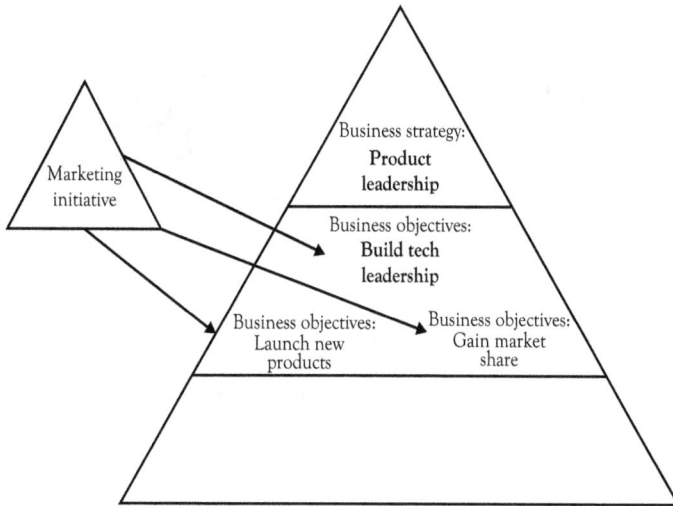

Figure 10.3 The combination of business strategy and business objectives goes right at the top of the pyramid

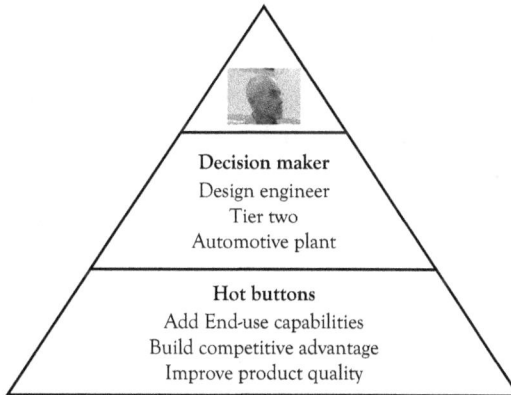

Figure 10.4 Summarize the audience, identifying the decision maker and their hot buttons

Second, Who Are You Talking to?

Next, you'll want to remind your managers who the target audience is. Following the process noted in Part II, you'll summarize the audience as shown in Figure 10.4. Those hot button concerns will figure prominently in later stages.

Three, What Are You Saying?

Then, following the process outlined in Part III, you'll add the core idea for your marketing initiative (shown in Figure 10.5). Needless to say, your core idea should address at least one of the audience hot buttons identified for the target personal. And it should be apparent how it will reinforce at least one of the business objectives.

Fourth, How Do You Reach Them?

Next, you'll walk through your media choices, as noted in Part IV, organizing the tactics (as in Figure 10.6).

You may need to point out the decision to organize the marketing tactics into campaigns. That only campaigns, not tactics, produce leads and sales. And that campaigns can be better optimized and leverage the cumulative impact of all your marketing efforts.

Fifth: How Will You Know If You're Successful?

Finally, as shown in Figure 10.7, you'll want to show how you optimized your campaign, using the tools in Chapter 9.

Then, after you've fully optimized the results, you'll want to update the KPIs on the right and add in the expenditures on the left to calculate the ROI (shown in Figure 10.8).

Core idea
No one makes
a better widget

Reasons to believe
• Advanced technology
• Product quality
• Applications expertise

Figure 10.5 Then add the messaging, the core idea, and the reasons to believe

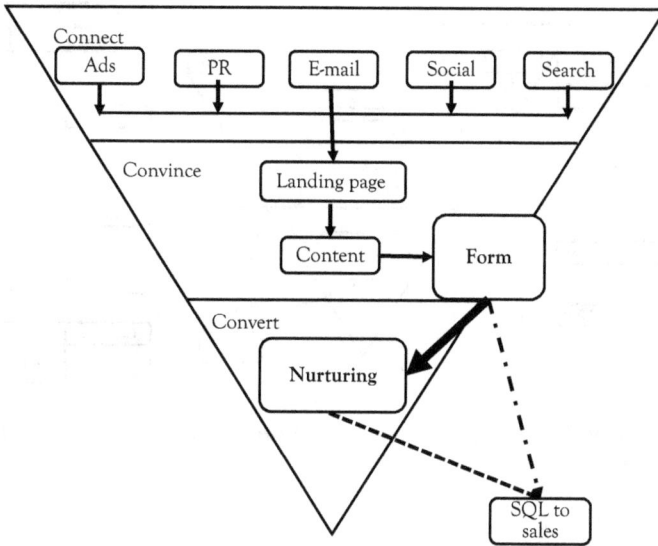

Figure 10.6 Add in the communications tools, including your media choices. Then show how the pieces all combine into a campaign

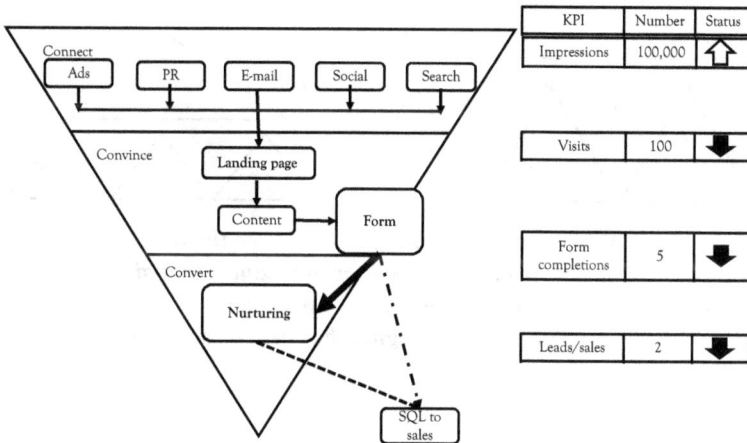

Figure 10.7 Indicate the tools you use to measure the success of each stage and optimize your campaign

Long-Term Brand Building

You can factor in long-term brand building as well (shown in Figure 10.9). What happens when you turn off brand advertising, social media, or PR? The answer: The performance of the entire campaign declines.

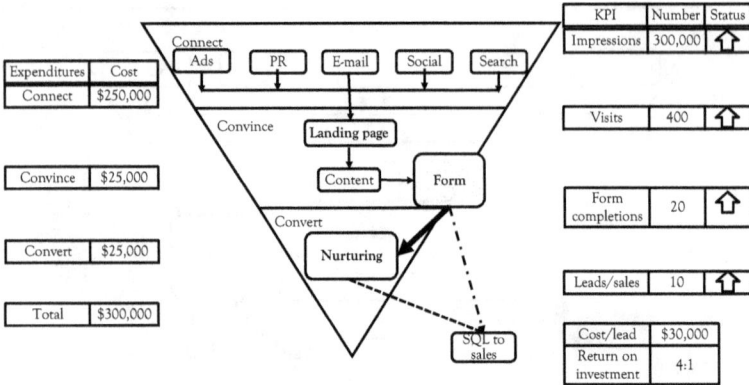

Figure 10.8 Finally, add in the expenditures and calculate the return on investment

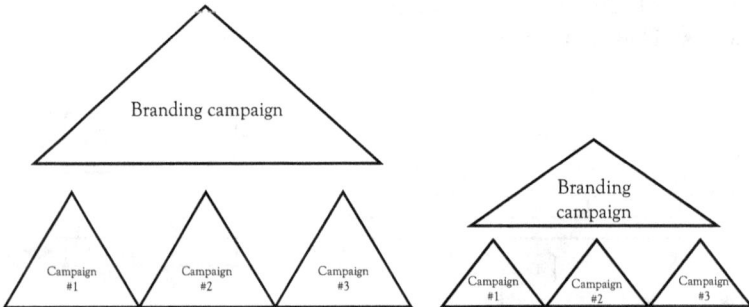

Figure 10.9 While some are too impatient to see the benefits of a branding campaign, it's not unusual for individual campaigns to shrink or flourish, depending on the resources devoted to a branding campaign. By tracking all campaigns, that benefit can be documented

Putting It All Together

Finally, combining the top and bottom sections, you'll have a single-page ROI dashboard (shown in Figure 10.10) that covers everything from business strategy, audience, and messaging to campaign planning, media choices, optimization, and ROI. Appendix B contains a template to develop a *Brand Vision* ROI dashboard.

The ROI Dashboard

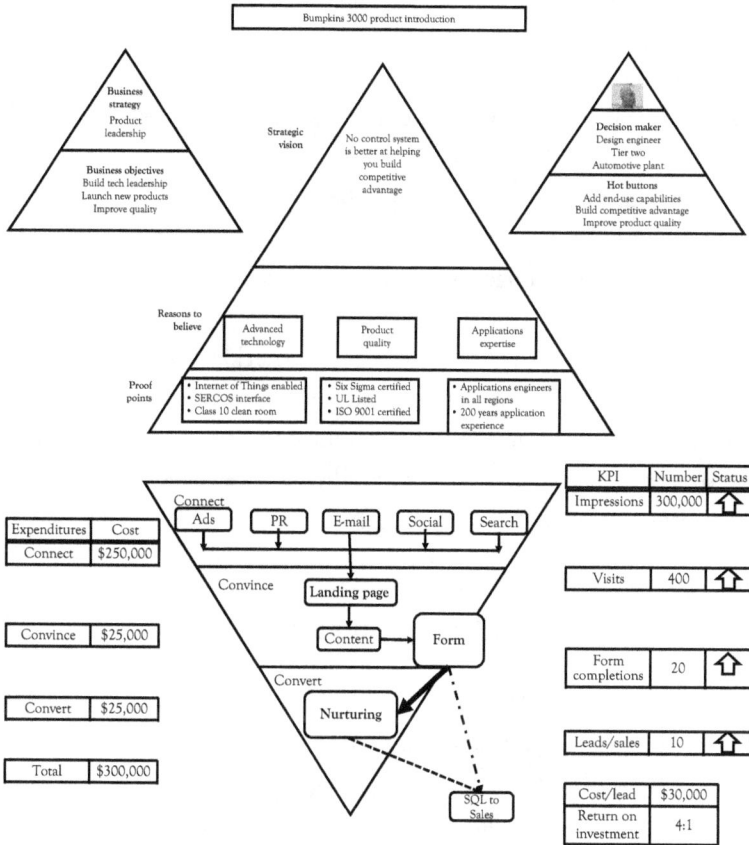

Figure 10.10 Using fictional numbers, this model assumes a 50 percent sales conversion rate for a sales qualified lead and a lifetime customer value of $120,000

What If the Client Wants to See Behind the Curtain?

What if the business leader or client wants to see how a tactic like a tweet or a Facebook post is doing? The short answer is "it's doing as expected."

The long answer is that, as noted before, we're not tracking individual tactics. What we are doing is exploiting each medium to its fullest. And all the tactics are being orchestrated to achieve maximum benefit for the campaign.

If at first, they weren't working as well as they should, they've been improved or optimized. And if they still aren't working, they have been eliminated.

It's all about finding the right mix of tactics for a specific campaign, then optimizing the hell out of it until it's performing as well as it can.

Most marketers really don't have enough experience to say what the best mix of tactics is, when they're just beginning to use the process. But that will come. And after as short a period as two years, a marketer's experience will be deep enough that they will be able to cite data about what we should be expecting from individual tactics.

In short, what management will really see quickly if they peek behind the curtain is a dedicated team of creatives and media specialists whose understanding of the audience and command of the media far exceeds the concerns management may have. They are way beyond a top-level skepticism, as they should be.

Chapter Summary

Points to Remember

- Calculating ROI is an elusive goal.
- Knowing what works in marketing is a game changer.
- An ROI report should be distributed to top management.

Advancing Brand Vision

Like it or not, calculating ROI is the icing on the cake for top management. It shows that marketers are willing to examine their work with a critical eye and learn from past mistakes. And it could well create a role for marketing, not just as a cost center, or even as a revenue generator. But as a way to anticipate the success of future efforts. And, thereby, earn a seat at the table.

Closing Thoughts

We began with strategy, introducing the idea of positioning and explaining the importance of business strategy to the marketing process.

We then talked about the audience, laying out the role that good audience insight and research plays in understanding the motivations and needs of our target audiences.

Next, we discussed messaging and the value of storytelling, explaining how to create a clear strategic vision, as well as content and creative that have impact.

Then we surveyed the media landscape and reviewed ways to organize the plethora of choices into campaigns that deliver.

And finally, we discussed measurement and the data collection that can help us optimize our campaigns for maximum impact and go to our C-level masters with compelling proof that their marketing dollars were well spent.

The goal? To tie marketing closely to strategy. Elevate the understanding of buying dynamics. Develop solid content and storylines. Cut through all the chaos and confusion in selecting media. Crunch the data to improve campaign performance and generate reliable ROI information. And ultimately, to provide corporate leaders with a clear line of sight connecting business strategy with marketing tactics.

That's the *Brand Vision* process. Designed to guide marketers through the chaos. Create a common language to improve internal communications. End debates about aesthetics. Make the best use of the reams of data available. Maximize their company's marketing investment. And allow marketing to be viewed as an important strategic capability, gaining a seat at the table when key decisions are made.

But most importantly, the goal of *Brand Vision* is to liberate marketers from the limitations, often self-imposed, that prevent them from reaching greater heights. Encourage them to keep asking questions, refining their tools, failing faster, and incorporating continuous improvement throughout the marketing process.

In short, to reach for the stars.

Appendix A

The Brand Vision Creative Brief

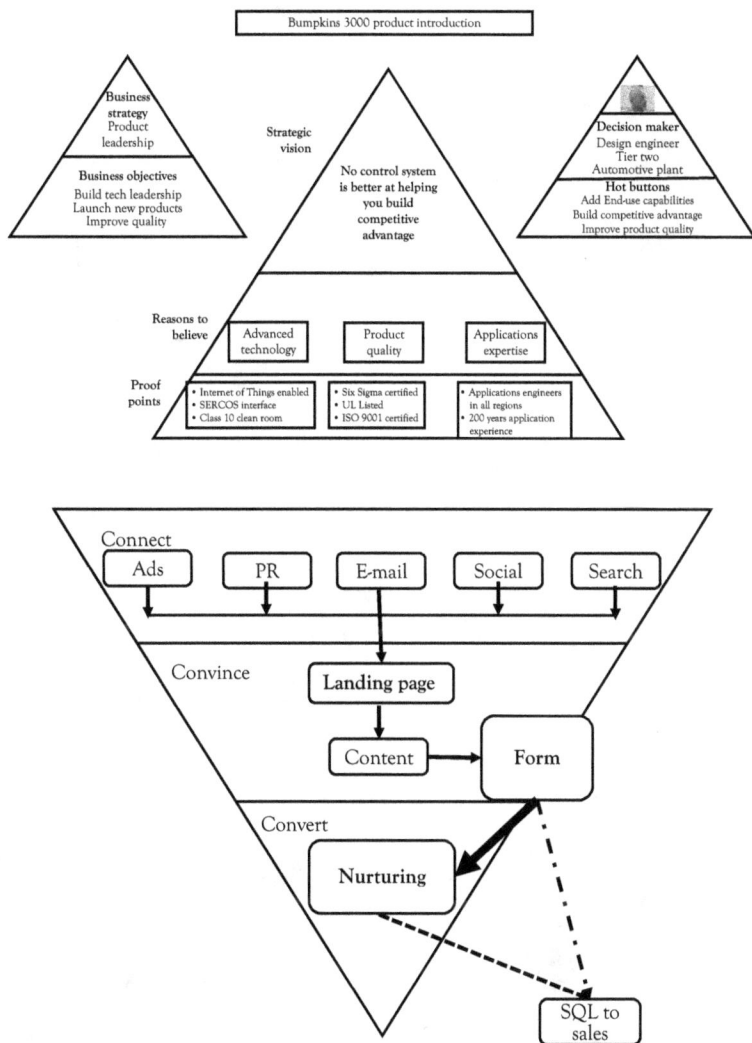

Figure A.1 The Brand Vision creative brief

Appendix B

The Brand Vision ROI Dashboard

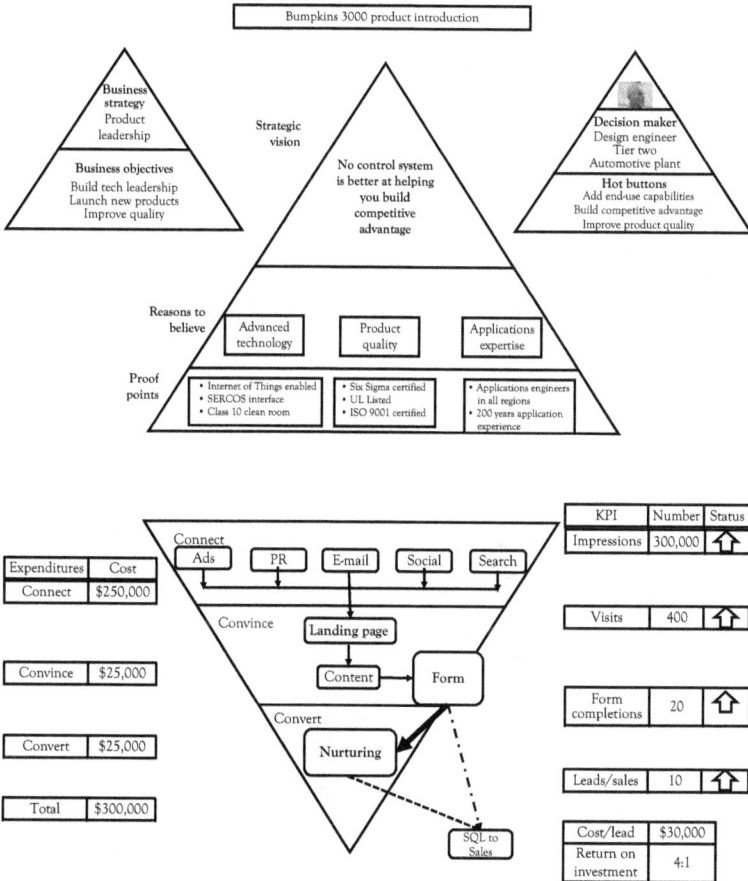

Figure B.1 The Brand Vision ROI dashboard

Bibliography

Anderson, J.C., N. Kumar, and J. Narus. 2007. *Value Merchants: Demonstrating and Documenting Superior Value in Business Markets.* Boston, MA: Harvard Business Review Press.

Anderson, J.C., J.A. Narus, and W. van Rossum. 2006. "Customer Value Propositions in Business Markets." In *HBR's 10 Must Reads on Strategic Marketing (with Featured Article "Marketing Myopia," by T. Levitt).* Boston: Harvard Business Review Press. Kindle Edition.

Christensen, C. 1997. *The Innovator's Dilemma: The Revolutionary Bestseller That Changed the Way We Do Business.* New York, NY: HarperCollins Publishers Inc.

Christensen, C.M., M.E. Raynor, and R. McDonald. December 2015. "What Is Disruptive Innovation?" *Harvard Business Review,* pp. 44–53.

Collins, J.C., and J.I. Porras. 1996. "Building Your Company's Vision." In *HBR's 10 Must Reads on Strategy (Including Featured Article "What Is Strategy?" by M.E. Porter).* Boston: Harvard Business Review Press, Kindle Edition.

Collins, J. 2011. *Good to Great.* New York, NY: Harper Business.

Denning, S. December 2015. "Fresh Insights From Clayton Christensen on Disruptive Innovation." *Forbes.* www.forbes.com/sites/stevedenning/2015/12/02/fresh-insights-from-clayton-christensen-on-disruptive-innovation/?sh=2de236854702 (accessed February 2016).

Elberse, A. 2011. "The Creative Industries: Managing and Marketing Talent, Module Note." *Harvard Business School.* https://hbsp.harvard.edu/product/509078-PDF-ENG

Finite and 93x. 2020. "The B2B Content Marketing Report." https://finite.cogniclick.app/report/12884cab7

Gadiesh, O., and J.L. Gilbert. 2001. "Transforming Corner-Office Strategy into Frontline Action." In *HBR's 10 Must Reads on Strategy (Including featured article "What Is Strategy?" by M.E. Porter).* Boston: Harvard Business Review Press. Kindle Edition.

Greyser, S.A., and R.F. Young. 1994. "Cunard Line Ltd.: Managing Integrated Marketing Communications." *Harvard Business School.* https://hbsp.harvard.edu/product/594046-PDF-ENG

Griffin, A., and J.R. Hauser. 2001. "The Voice of the Customer." *Marketing Science* 22, no. 1, pp. 1–27.

Gupta, S. 2018. *Driving Digital Strategy: A Guide to Reimagining Your Business, 9. Measuring and Optimizing Marketing Spend.* Boston, MA: Harvard Business Press Books.

Hambrick, D.C., and J.W. Fredrickson. 2001. "Are you Sure You have a Strategy?" *Academy of Management Executive* 15, no. 4, pp. 48–59.

Hamel, G., and M. Zanini. 2020. *Humanocracy: Creating Organizations as Amazing as the People Inside Them.* Boston, MA: Harvard Business School Publishing.

Hubbard, T.N., P. Leinwand, and C. Mainardi. Autumn 2014. "The New Supercompetitors." *Strategy + Business.* www.strategy-business.com/article/00272 (accessed March 2016).

Joly, H. 2021. *The Heart of Business: Leadership Principles for the Next Era of Capitalism.* Boston, MA: Harvard Business Review Press.

Kim, W.C., and R. Mauborgne. 2015. *Blue Ocean Shift: Proven Steps to Inspire Confidence and Seize New Growth.* New York, NY: Hachette Books.

Kim, W.C., and R. Mauborgne. 2015. *Blue Ocean Strategy: How to Create Uncontested Market Space and Make the Competition Irrelevant.* Boston, MA: Harvard Business School Publishing.

Levinson, J.C. 2006. *Guerilla Marketing: Put Your Advertising on Steroids!* Garden City, NY: Morgan James Publishing, LLC.

Mankins, M.C., and R. Steele. 2005. "Turning Great Strategy into Great Performance." In *HBR's 10 Must Reads on Strategy (Including Featured Article "What Is Strategy?" by M.E. Porter).* Boston: Harvard Business Review Press. Kindle Edition.

Moore, G.A. 1991. *Crossing the Chasm: Marketing and Selling High-Tech Products to Mainstream Consumers.* New York, NY: HarperCollins Publishers Inc.

Moore, G.A. 2000. *Living on the Fault Line: Managing for Shareholder Value in the Age of the Internet.* New York, NY: HarperCollins Publishers Inc.

Neilson, G.L., K.L. Martin, and E. Powers. 2008. "The Secrets to Successful Strategy Execution." In *HBR's 10 Must Reads on Strategy (Including Featured Article "What Is Strategy?" by M.E. Porter).* Boston: Harvard Business Review Press. Kindle Edition.

Porter, M.E. 1980. *Competitive Strategy: Techniques for Analyzing Industries and Competitors.* New York, NY: The Free Press.

Porter, M.E., and J.E. Heppelman. November 2014. "How Smart, Connected Products Are Transforming Competition." *Harvard Business Review,* https://hbr.org/2014/11/how-smart-connected-products-are-transforming-competition (accessed December 2014).

Reichheld, F.F. 2003. "The One Number You Need to Grow." In *HBR's 10 Must Reads on Strategic Marketing (with featured article "Marketing Myopia," by T. Levitt),* 151–169. Boston: Harvard Business Review Press. Kindle Edition.

Reinartz, W., and P. Saffert. June 2013. "Creativity in Advertising: When It Works and When It Doesn't." *Harvard Business Review.* https://hbr.org/2013/06/creativity-in-advertising-when-it-works-and-when-it-doesnt?autocomplete=true (accessed December 2013).

Ries, A., and J. Trout. 2006. *Marketing Warfare.* New York, NY: McGraw Hill Companies, Inc.

Rogers, P., and M. Blenko. 2006. "Who Has the D? How Clear Decision Roles Enhance Organizational Performance. In *HBR's 10 Must Reads on Strategy (including featured article "What Is Strategy?" by M.E. Porter).* Boston: Harvard Business Review Press. Kindle Edition.

Rust, R.T., C. Moorman, and G. Bhalla. 2010. "Rethinking Marketing." In *HBR's 10 Must Reads on Strategic Marketing (with featured article "Marketing Myopia," by T. Levitt).* Boston: Harvard Business Review Press. Kindle Edition.

Sawhney, M., and M. Biddlecom, R. Day, P. Franke, J. Lee-Tin, R. Leonard, and B. Poger. 2004. "Rockwell Automation: The Channel Challenge." *Kellogg School of Management.* https://hbsp.harvard.edu/product/KEL163-PDF-ENG?Ntt=marketing%20through%20distributors

Schultz, R. 2020. "The Gate Swings Both Ways: Don't Make It Too Hard to Access B2B Content." *MediaPost.* www.mediapost.com/publications/article/357436/the-gate-swings-both-ways-dont-make-it-too-hard.html

Sitecore. 2016. "What Is Omnichannel and Why Should We Be Doing It?"

Taylor, M., and M. Vandenbosch. n.d. "Bolster Electronics: Dealing with Dealer Demands." *Ivey Publishing.* https://hbsp.harvard.edu/product/W12242-PDF-ENG?Ntt=marketing%20through%20distributors

TechTarget. 2018. "Why B2B Marketers Can't Afford to Ignore Digital Advertising." www.techtarget.com/resources/why-b2b-marketers-cant-afford-to-ignore-digital-advertising/

Treacy, M., and F. Wiersma. 1995. *The Discipline of Market Leaders: Choose Your Customers, Narrow Your Focus, Dominate Your Market.* Reading, MA: Addison-Wesley Publishing Company.

Wessel, M., and C.M. Christensen. 2012. "Surviving Disruption." In *HBR's 10 Must Reads on Strategy, Vol. 2 (with bonus article "Creating Shared Value" By M.E. Porter and M.R. Kramer).* Boston: Harvard Business Review Press. Kindle Edition.

Zook, C., and J. Allen. 2011. "The Great Repeatable Business Model." In *HBR's 10 Must Reads on Strategy, Vol. 2 (with bonus article "Creating Shared Value" By M.E. Porter and M.R. Kramer).* Boston: Harvard Business Review Press. Kindle Edition.

About the Author

Jim Everhart is a freelance strategist and writer, working with corporations and agencies to develop marketing communications tactics and campaigns. He spent more than four decades in the marketing industry, most of it at Godfrey Advertising, one of the largest business-to-business marketing agencies in the United States. He played a leadership role at Godfrey in marketing strategy, technology development, and creative implementation, rising to the position of vice president and creative director.

Index